# Declarations
of a
# Dinosaur

# Declarations
## of a
# Dinosaur

## 10 LAWS I'VE LEARNED
## AS A FAMILY DOCTOR

*Lucy E. Hornstein, MD*

To Andrew,

With fond memories of TBTF.

Lucy Hornstein

September 2013

**KAPLAN**

PUBLISHING

New York

Published by Kaplan Publishing, a division of Kaplan, Inc.
1 Liberty Plaza, 24th Floor
New York, NY 10006

Library of Congress Cataloging-in-Publication Data
has been applied for.

Printed in the United States of America

10 9 8 7 6 5 4 3 2 1

ISBN13: 978-1-4277-9870-1

Kaplan Publishing books are available at special quantity discounts to use for sales promotions, employee premiums, or educational purposes. Please email our Special Sales Department to order or for more information at kaplanpublishing@kaplan.com, or write to Kaplan Publishing, 1 Liberty Plaza, 24th Floor, New York, NY 10006.

*To GHS, father and friend;*

*All my love, always.*

# Table of Contents

The art of medicine consists of amusing the
patient while nature takes its course.

It is impossible to make an asymptomatic patient
feel better.

The urgency of the test is inversely proportional to the
IQ of the insurance company pre-authorization clerk.

There is no cure for stupid.

Bad things really do happen to good people.

The better the surgeon, the more reluctant
he is to operate.

# Acknowledgments

NO MAN (OR WOMAN) is an island, and no book is created alone. I would therefore like to thank some of the myriad others who have had a hand in this little volume.

The Internet is a funny place, where real and surreal blend until the lines between them blur into oblivion. Those who blog are special people, and it is thrilling to convert the faceless names behind the words into actual friends. Thanks to the Tundra PA, Ambulance Driver, Cranky Professor, Moof, Medblog Addict, TeenDoc, and all the other pseudonymous bloggers, along with Kevin, Sid, Peggy, Lynn, and the rest who blog with their actual names, for supporting my blogging. This is all your fault, you know.

Special thanks to Michael Sprague for prowling around the blogs and inviting me to expound on the Laws of the Dinosaur, as well as Kim Bowers and everyone else at Kaplan Publishing for this fantastic opportunity.

"Thanks" doesn't begin to appropriately express my appreciation for the world's greatest agent, Janet Reid, and the fine folk at FinePrint Literary.

Thanks to my kids, Matt, Joanna, Ben, and Lindsay. Just because you're out of the house doesn't mean you're not on my mind (even though I have to admit it's much easier to write when you're out of the house). (Just kidding.) Love you all.

Last but never least, my most Darling Spouse, who saw way too much of my back as I slaved away at the family room computer, oblivious to such trivial endeavors as sleeping and house cleaning. Thank you, Bill.

# Preamble to
## *Declarations of a Dinosaur*

ONCE UPON A TIME there was a little girl who wanted to be a doctor. Her parents, who were almost as smart as she, said, "That's nice," and waited for her to change her mind. She never did. Instead, she began deliberating about what specific field of medicine was calling to her. She read voraciously: *The Making of a Surgeon* by William Nolan, which introduced her to surgery; *Intern* by Dr. X, describing the rotating internship. And then just as the girl's childhood was morphing into adolescence, a character burst onto the small screen: television's Marcus Welby, MD, played by none other than that Best-Knowing Father himself, Robert Young.

Marcus Welby was a suburban family doctor. He did everything, taking care of children, adults, and old folks; heart disease, skin disease, and psychiatric disease. And he did it with warmth, kindness, and panache, in a lovely stone ranch house with a home office. Although money was never seen changing hands, he obviously made a comfortable living—as did his sidekick, heartthrob Dr. Steven Kiley (played by a pre-Streisand James Brolin), who drove one sharp motor-cycle. The girl was hooked; *that's* the kind of doctor she was going to be. Perhaps it wouldn't be the most lucrative of careers, but money wasn't the point. It was all about the dream. Just like Marcus Welby, MD—and most of the physicians she met over the years—she just wanted to practice without worrying about the business side of medicine. At the very least, it seemed she would certainly never starve.

Time passed, as it is wont to do. The girl, now a young woman, graduated from high school the year after the television show "Marcus Welby, MD" was cancelled, and she proceeded through college and medical school, never wavering in her commitment to the idea of family practice. Her three years of residency training were appropriately grueling, interrupted by a five-month maternity leave to deliver twins. By the time she finished her training, she was pregnant with her third child. After he was born, she went looking for a place to hang out her shingle. After all these years, her dream was coming true at last.

Things went well at first. Patients flocked to her door and fell in love with her down-to-earth style of practice. They marveled that she didn't speak medical jargon to them. They marveled that she didn't take Wednesdays off. They marveled that they could read her handwriting. They told her she wasn't like any other doctor they had ever met, and she reveled in their affection.

Certainly the business of medicine had changed in

the years between the time Marcus Welby's shingle had gone off the air and hers had gone up. Third-party payers had become the rule rather than the exception. Instead of patients paying the doctor directly for her services, the modern expectation was that their employers would pay premiums to health insurance companies which, in turn, contracted with her and other physicians and hospitals to pay for the patients' medical care. The original concept was the insurance companies' promise that an increased volume of patients to contracted doctors would offset the discounted fees they requested. The young doctor made out well enough at the beginning, even though there wasn't much negotiation involved in those contracts by the time she began her practice. At that point even the smallest insurance company had much more bargaining power than any solo doctor, so her choices were limited to "take it" or "leave it." Still, the first seven years weren't bad, and her income gradually increased.

Then the business model shifted again. Driven primarily by a few entrepreneurial physicians (of all people), the concept of prepaid healthcare arose. Instead of paying a doctor for a visit by a patient, the idea was to predict what care a patient would need in a given year, calculate what the insurance company was willing to pay for it, divide that figure into twelve parts, and pay that amount to the doctor each month. The idea behind "paying by the head," or capitation, was to shift the financial risk from the insurance company to the doctor. If a patient came in ten times in one month, under the pay-per-visit scheme the insurance company would be on the hook for the cost. With capitation the doctor took the hit. To the extent that doctors kept the patients healthy—and out of the office—they could clean up. In theory, it sounded fair. The difficulties came with the implementation: two of the stickiest problems were patients who switched doctors before the year was up, and the appropriate setting of the rates. Other issues that conspired to sink the concept over the next decade included referrals, a mechanism that forced patients to visit their family doctors before they could see specialists. Although this is generally a good idea in medical practice, the prospect of being required to do something rarely sits well with Americans.

Throughout this period the role of the insurance companies expanded, becoming more intrusive as they insinuated themselves into the relationship between the doctor and her patients. They tried to tell her what drugs she should and shouldn't prescribe, and what tests she should and shouldn't order. Worst of all, not only did the companies' payment rates fail to keep pace with the cost of living, they either remained the same or decreased. Because all of the doctor's other costs kept increasing, her net income decreased. But her patients still loved her, and she cared deeply for them. And she wasn't starving. Yet. So she stayed the course, even as each year became more difficult than the one before.

Computers became more common over the years, both

in homes and in medical offices. The Internet became a resource to access medical information when the doctor needed to research a problem for a patient, and later was an opportunity for social networking. Not surprisingly, other doctors were facing the same problems as she. However, because of these and other issues, she discovered that fewer and fewer of her colleagues were choosing to go it alone like she and Marcus Welby did. Worse, the number of medical students opting to train as family physicians was plummeting, almost certainly because income expectations were continuing to decrease. How could young men and women starting out with six figures of medical school debt commit to a career that wouldn't allow them to make enough money to pay it back, much less provide for themselves and their families? Although the doctor wasn't old by any means, she began to sense that her beloved profession and her chosen style of practice were on the verge of extinction.

She began to keep an online diary; a blog, on which she assumed the identity of *#1 Dinosaur*, hoping against hope that she wouldn't truly turn out to be the last of her kind. She used the blog to broadcast the trials and tribulations, along with the joys and triumphs, of solo family practice in the 21st century to anyone who would read. She made friends and influenced people, including nurses, paramedics, pharmacists, medical students, other doctors, patients, and many others. Along the way, she accumulated snarky snippets of wisdom about medical practice—equal parts borrowed, adapted, and invented—and codified them on the sidebar of her blog as THE LAWS OF THE DINO- SAUR. Though often expressed humorously, each Law contained a seed of great truth about the present state of medical practice in America. In the fullness of time, she had the extreme good fortune to have the opportunity to expand upon each of these Laws, allowing a unique glimpse into the possibly disappearing world of the solo family phy- sician of today. That girl who became a doctor was me, your author; and this view—the result of all that experience, observation, concentration, and collaboration—is what you hold in your hand.

# The art of medicine consists of amusing the patient while nature takes its course.

"TREATING AN ABSCESS with antibiotics is like pissing into the ocean and expecting the tide to rise."

The distinguished surgeon addressing my second-year medical school class was simply imparting a piece of basic surgical wisdom: In the presence of infection, the body responds with inflammation. White blood cells congregate, consuming invading bacteria, destroying devitalized tissue, and walling off the area to prevent the infection from spreading. Early in the process, antibiotic drugs that kill the germs can be helpful; sometimes curative. But by the time the whole mess of bacteria, white cells, and dead tissue has liquefied into that distinctively scented, deceptively creamy, yellow-green substance known as pus, all you can do is drain it. That huge, intensely painful, angry red lump on butt or back or leg or wherever isn't going anywhere on its own. It must be laid wide open with a cold steel blade, and the cavity probed with finger or instrument to break up any loculations that may be sequestering pockets of pus. The infection eventually heals from the inside out, but the surgeons also taught that if the wound closes over too quickly the pus can re-accumulate, effectively negating all previous efforts. Thus, once it's drained, the abscess cavity has to be filled with packing; yards of gauze tape painstakingly folded into the now-gaping hole, and left for 24 hours. From my patients' reactions, I couldn't tell which was worse: the incision and drainage procedure itself or the removal of the packing the next day.

But the surgeons said this was what needed to happen, and I learned and obeyed—even though Marcus Welby never had to deal with pus.

After I'd been in practice for a few years, a woman came to see me with an abscess in her groin. The diagnosis was not in question. She had a hot, red, swollen lump, soft where the tissue had begun to liquefy into pus. According to the patient, it also hurt like hell. It was big enough that I didn't feel comfortable performing the I&D in my office. But this was an abscess and it needed to be drained.

"You need to see the surgeon," I intoned. "That needs to be drained."

"Oh, I can't," answered the patient. "I have to get back to work. Why don't you just give me some antibiotics and I'll be fine."

"But... but... it's an abscess," I sputtered. "The surgeons say it has to be drained. Writing a prescription would be like throwing antibiotics into the ocean and expecting piss to come in with the tide. Or something like that."

The patient remained serene.

"Oh no, I get these all the time. I just need some antibiotics."

"Won't you *please* go see the surgeon?"

"No."

There it was. All I could do was write the antibiotic prescription, and off she went, happy as a clam. A clam in some fairly significant pain, but happy.

I truly believed this woman would be calling me back in a few days, contrite. She would tell me she was no better and was now ready to accept my recommendation for surgical drainage. I couldn't figure out what I had done wrong. Patients always did what Marcus Welby told them to do.

A day passed. Then another. Soon it was a week; then another. The most likely scenario was that she had gone to an Emergency Room to have it taken care of when the pain grew unbearable, too embarrassed to come back to me for the implicit "I told you so." A few months later I saw the woman's name on the schedule again. Aha! I thought; she'd tried the antibiotic but the tide of piss had gone out, or something like that.

Imagine my surprise, though, when I entered the exam room and she began complaining about a cough.

"What?" I asked.

"I have a cough," she said.

"Why would an abscess in your groin give you a cough?" I wondered aloud.

Her laugh tinkled like piss in the ocean.

"Oh, that!" she answered. "That went away just fine with the antibiotic. I've had a cough for three days now."

"What?" I was astonished. "Without being drained? It just went away?"

"Well, I did use the antibiotic," she responded. "I also put a hot washcloth on it. It burst on its own and I squeezed all this nasty stinky green stuff out of it. Then it healed up."

"But … but … it's not supposed to do that," was all I could say.

"Well, it did. Now what about my cough?"

That was the first time I saw an abscess that wasn't supposed to respond to antibiotics do just that, though it wasn't the last. It turns out that the hot compresses are the trick. When the skin over an abscess is heated, the capillaries dilate and bring more blood to the surface. The white cells eat away at the skin, thinning it until a hole forms and the pus drains on its own. All I have to do is humor the patient with an antibiotic prescription and even an abscess can run its course. Who knew? Did Marcus Welby?

NATURE GENERALLY takes its course. Always has; always will. Nowhere is this truth more self-evident than with the common cold. There is nothing I can do for a cold. Nothing. Really—nothing at all. Why don't people believe me?

"Doctor, I've had a runny nose since yesterday."

"I've had a fever all weekend."

"Doc, my throat has been killing me for three days."

"This cough is driving me crazy."

Each of these complaints is invariably followed by one of these comments:

"I have to be on a plane tomorrow."

"There's no one else to take care of my kids."

"We're leaving on vacation at the end of the week."

"My mother-in-law is coming to visit and I can't be sick."

"I can't be sick."

"I can't be sick."

"I can't be sick."

Somehow, my advice to rest, drink plenty of fluids, and allow the virus to run its course always falls on deaf ears—or maybe just ears with fluid accumulated behind the eardrums, which muffles their hearing. And so I am cast into the role of magician:

"You have to do something."

"I have to get better."

"You have to give me something."

"You have to make me better."

If it's magic they want, then magic I deliver.

Stacked in the drawers in my exam rooms are some slender wooden sticks I don't use anymore. Back in the olden days (i.e., before 1995), the Papanicolaou test for cervical cancer—the Pap smear—was really a smear. We scraped the uterine cervix gently with a specially shaped wooden spatula to collect cells for microscopic examination, then physically smeared those cells onto a glass slide. Technique mattered. The smear couldn't be too thick or too thin, and you had to spray it with fixative before it dried on its own. There were all kinds of other little details to remember too: for instance, you had to use a pencil to write the patient's name on the slide. If you used a pen by mistake, the fixative dissolved the ink, causing it to run right into the specimen. This created two messes: one on the slide and another when you told the patient you had to repeat the procedure to get more cells.

In the fullness of time, a new technique was developed: cells were obtained with a plastic spatula instead of a wooden one and were deposited into a small vial of fluid. The lab then created the slides themselves, absolving me from blame for technical failures. The major downside was the stash of now-useless wooden spatulas still haunting a drawer in each exam room, along with the big box of them left over in the cupboard.

I'll never forget the first time my "magical" idea occurred to me. A businessman sat before me, deep in the throes of an upper respiratory infection whose course I was powerless to affect. Still, he was insistent.

"Doc, I need to be on that plane tomorrow and I need you to make me well right away!"

I sighed deeply. Then I reached into the drawer and pulled out one of the old wooden cervical scrapers, hoping against hope that he didn't recognize what it really was. I took my pen and began writing along the shaft. When I was done, I showed him what I had engraved:

"Magic Get Well Right Away Stick."

I took the wand from him and stepped back.

"Okay," I said, "Get ready."

I rolled my head around, loosening up my shoulders like a pitcher in the bullpen. Then I raised my arm and rotated the tip of the stick a few times in the air as if gathering the magic around it like cotton candy. Finally, I gave it a mighty flick in his direction. I put my arm down and peered at the patient.

He was writhing with laughter.

"Are you better yet?" I asked.

It took a moment for him to collect himself.

"Okay, okay, Doc. I get the point."

"Here," I said, handing him the stick. "In case you need another dose later."

GERM THEORY is really cool; without a doubt one of the greatest scientific advances of all time. Discovered by Louis Pasteur, their relationship to disease formalized by Robert Koch, and their eradication promoted by Lister and Semmelweis, germs have a long and celebrated history with humankind. Many infectious diseases have been effectively vanquished, including smallpox, plague, and yellow fever. The eradication of too many others—measles, mumps, polio—remains a technically attainable goal, except in populations who are unable or unwilling to participate in such basic programs as sanitation and immunization. Although there are still some people in this day and age who reject the germ theory, germs don't care; much the same way that people who do not believe in the theory of gravity don't fall off the planet.

There are different kinds of germs that cause different kinds of diseases, some of which can be treated and some of which cannot—despite all the wishing and hoping and demanding that the American public can muster.

Bacteria are single-celled organisms that peaceably colonize much of the human body, where they number in the trillions. They nestle themselves into accommodating spots, squeezing through the most minute of breaks in the skin or mucous membranes. Like any other cell, they consume nutrients, excrete wastes, and metabolize to their little mitochondria's content. Some even move—those equipped with subcellular fins and propellers, known respectively as cilia and flagella. They also reproduce: in the M phase, when a young unicellular organism's fancy turns to thoughts of mitosis, they get plump and juicy enough to split into two, each cell growing and enlarging on its own, as the cell cycle of life goes on.

In this way bacteria multiply, never caring if some of their metabolites just happen to shut down the organs of the human body as they circulate through it. One by one, liver, lungs, kidneys, and heart fail in the face of overwhelming bacterial sepsis. Oh, the germs can be killed; poisoned with drugs known as antibiotics that interfere with bacterial metabolism in dozens of different ways. But over millennia of generations to them—a time frame as little as a few years to us—bacteria grow and evolve and develop in new ways, now resistant to the poisons. This is why the predictions of bacterial extinction at the beginning of the antibiotic age were so premature. Bacteria were here long before us, and chances are pretty good that they'll outlast the last of us, laughing all the way.

Viruses, on the other hand, aren't even cells. No plasma membrane, no cytoplasm, no nucleus, no ribosomes, no mitochondria, none of it. Too small even to be seen with a regular microscope, a virus is nothing more than a tiny package of genetic material tucked into a little protein coat. Some species, such as human immunodeficiency virus (HIV), include a special enzyme or two within its protein envelope. Its mission—which it frequently chooses to accept—is to attach to a cell in order to gain entry for its genetic material. Once inside, the nucleic acid strand hijacks the cell's metabolic machinery, forcing its protein-producing ribosomes to make viral proteins. Under viral influence, the cell's nucleus is coerced into reproducing the genes of the invader. The hostage cell then has to assemble the viral genome and protein coat into complete virions. The cell eventually bursts when it can no longer contain the packed viral clones, releasing them into the world of the body, each virion to set off in search of new cells to infect.

Not all viruses kill the cells they infect. Some of them have the capability of inserting their genetic material into the cell's chromosomes, thus effectively lengthening their lifespan by allowing them to reproduce themselves along with the cell. This is how certain DNA viruses such as herpesviruses and human papillomavirus manage to stick around and cause much of their mischief.

But the tiny RNA viruses that cause the common cold aren't so smart. They love to insinuate themselves into the epithelial cells lining the nose, throat, and airways that lead to the lungs, destroying cells with abandon as the surrounding tissue swells, bringing white blood cells to the area to oust the invaders. Who cares if they leave your nose so stuffed that you can't breathe through it? They're busy fighting infection! Another strategy is to turn the heat up, because cells don't work as well at higher temperatures.

Running a fever makes the virus less efficient at reproducing itself, eventually killing it; much like sabotage from the resistance in World War II France. Not that the body cares about the headaches and muscle pains and coughing that result from the fever and inflammation. Infection-fighting is serious business!

Still, the body knows what it's doing. Because the virus has actually invaded the body's cells, you can't really give any medicine that will kill the virus without damaging the host. (As it happens, there are some exceptions to this. Certain viruses can be "faked out." Providing them with defective building materials causes them to make faulty viral particles, thus hastening the end of the misery they cause. But no such drugs exist for the common cold and, because there are more than a thousand different cold viruses, it seems unlikely that any such medications will be developed.) The bottom line is that we humans are stuck with this universal, unalterable truth: there is nothing to do for the common cold except let it run its course. Which it will; no one ever dies of a cold per se. Some unfortunate souls develop complications, usually a bacterial invader that sees its chance to sneak into a body that's in a weakened state. But by and large, in the grand scheme of things, there is nothing I can do for patients who come to me with a cold.

Really. Nothing at all.

THERE ARE PLENTY of instances where patients get better without my actually doing anything. Ear infections in kids are one example.

Back in the day, a bright red eardrum was considered a sign of bacterial infection, so naturally the treatment was antibiotics. How else were the poor kids going to get better?

I never had reason to believe otherwise, until one Thursday afternoon when I saw a little boy with an ear infection. At least his mother had thought it was an ear infection on Wednesday. The kid had a fever and an earache, so that day the mother had called my office to schedule an appointment. As it happened, I didn't see the kid until 24 hours later. And wouldn't you know, his ear didn't hurt anymore and the fever was gone by then.

"So why did you bring him in?" I asked the mother.

"Well, we had the appointment."

Made as much sense as anything else.

But when I looked into the child's ear, the eardrum was still a bright, angry red and was bulging as if his brains were trying to squeeze their way out of his skull.

*Whoa*, I thought.

"Does your ear hurt?" I asked the kid.

"No."

"Really?"

"Yes."

Hmm.

I realized that if I had seen him 24 hours ago and had seen that clearly infected middle ear, I would have winced in sympathy as I wrote the poor kid his antibiotic prescription. Then, by today, the ear would have stopped hurting—because it had—and the mother, Marcus Welby, and I all would have chimed in together, "Isn't that antibiotic wonderful!"

Instead, I had chanced upon the discovery that the amoxicillin I would have prescribed wouldn't really have made any difference at all. More recently, it has been shown that most ear infections are in fact caused by viruses. Large studies have shown that antibiotics are best reserved for a subset of children who have fever and vomiting as symptoms of their ear infection.

"So what do we do for his ear?" asked the mom.

The truth was that I had no idea, but I decided to wing it. Since the ear had stopped hurting on its own, the red and bulging eardrum would most likely resolve spontaneously as well. No need to prescribe an unnecessary medication.

"Why don't you just give him pain medicine if his ear hurts, keep an eye on him, and call me back if anything changes," I said, figuring I'd covered pretty much every possibility.

"Sounds like a good idea. Thank you very much, Doctor."

"You're very welcome," I answered.

Marcus Welby would have been proud.

THE LONGER I PRACTICED, the better I got at amusing patients for whom there wasn't anything else I could do. One mother brought her baby girl in to see me because she was afraid the child had an ear infection.

"Why do you think she has an ear infection?" I asked.

"Because she's been playing with her ears," answered the mother.

"Anything else? Stuffy nose? Cough? Other cold symptoms?"

"No; she's just been playing with her ears."

"Both of them, or one more than the other?"

"That one," she said, pointing to the baby's left ear just as the little girl reached up and started pulling at her right ear.

"Okay," I said, flipping on my wall-mounted diagnostic set and lifting the otoscope from its cradle. I fitted it with a small plastic earpiece and examined the baby's ears.

The right one was perfect: no wax; the eardrum was pearly white, its landmarks clear. No infection.

Then the left: canal clear; eardrum pearly and perfect.

"No ear infection," I stated.

The mother wasn't impressed.

"Then why is she playing with her ear?"

The words popped out of my mouth almost before I realized I had thought them.

"Because she doesn't have a penis. What else is she going to play with?"

The mother's eyebrows disappeared into her hairline as she began to laugh uproariously.

"Doc," she wheezed, "you are too funny!"

She laughed all the way out the door, relieved about her daughter's ears.

THEN THERE WAS the call from the woman whose toddler had just swallowed a ball bearing.

A brief anatomy lesson: the human gastrointestinal (GI) tract is a tube that connects the mouth to the anus, and through that tube food flows like a mighty river. Boluses of food and drink pass into the throat and rush down the esophagus like a waterfall. They land in the stomach, where the GI tract widens and slows like the Hudson River at Tappan Zee. After being attacked by proteases and other enzymes that function in an environment more acidic than any other place known on earth, food exits the stomach through the narrow pylorus, much as the Mediterranean meets the Atlantic at Gibraltar; the food is now diluted and transformed into semi-liquid chyme. Next, it meanders around the hairpin turn of the duodenum, accepting a squirt of bile and pancreatic enzymes emerging from the sphincter of Oddi to help break down and digest the fatty components of the meal. The switchbacks continue through the small-bowel portions of jejunum and ileum, like the Mississippi wandering to its delta. The mucosal lining is velvety to the naked eye because the tissue is arranged in millions of tiny, finger-like villi, the better to increase its surface area available to absorb food, now broken down into its primary components of amino acids, small fragments of carbohydrates, fatty acids, and other compounds.

As nutrients are absorbed, all that is left are the waste products: the fiber and other non-absorbable components now stained with bile, still diluted in water. Through the final section of tortuous curves, the terminal ileum represents the small intestine's last chance to absorb essential vitamins and nutrients before the stream moves into the large intestine. The larger the passage, the slower the stream moves, like the wide calmness of the river once the rapids are behind. What's left of the meal moves slowly up the right, ascending to the liver, where the colon takes a sharp turn to the left. Traversing the abdomen, it reaches the spleen and takes another left, turning back down, the end now almost in sight. During its passage through the colon, the food-become-waste loses water, as the colon reclaims liquid for the body. As it dries, the waste becomes pasty, then formed, then firm. A few more gentle sigmoid curves and the stool is delivered into the rectum, where it awaits the call of nature. A final push, and it is flushed away to join yet another mighty stream.

The GI tract differs from a river in that food doesn't just move passively through it. Each section of the passage is a muscular tube, constricting and relaxing in precise coordination to move its contents along downstream. Just as other muscles in the body require nerves to translate the commands of the brain into movement, the muscles of the GI tract have their own intrinsic nervous system; a network of neurons and ganglia in a vast relay that maintains the flow. In a way, it can thus be said that the gut has a mind of its own. Just as in a river, though, anything that impedes the flow through the GI tract causes problems. Some causes of obstruction arise from within, like cancerous tumors of the colon that grow concentrically for years before finally pinching off the passage. But it is often the swallowing of an object that is too big or is irregularly shaped that causes problems, be it a hunk of meat someone was too hungry to chew properly or an inanimate object that doesn't belong in the mouth in the first place. Still, the muscles of the gut are amazingly strong, contracting involuntarily in waves of peristalsis capable of pushing quite a variety of swallowed flotsam safely through to the end. Small, smooth objects like ball bearings are a no-brainer for the GI tract as they slip through the esophagus into the stomach, around the curves of the small intestine, through the ileocecal valve into the colon and straight through into the toilet, possibly even with a satisfying "clink" on the porcelain.

Back to the patient: I knew the mother waited anxiously on the other end of the phone, and despite the fact that the swallowed foreign body represented no hazard to her child whatsoever, I sensed that the way I chose to present that information would determine how much reassurance I'd be able to convey. Suddenly, amazingly, the perfect words popped into my head fully formed. I took the opportunity to savor their brilliance as I pronounced slowly and carefully, "This, too, shall pass."

AH, BUT WHAT ABOUT all those other times when the patient really does need me to do something? When that murmur I hear turns out to be a damaged valve in the heart; or that bellyache is really an inflamed, infected appendix about to burst; or those hard, swollen glands in the neck mean cancer of the throat instead of just an upper respiratory infection? As Marcus Welby always said, medicine is both art and science; and these instances are the times to haul out the science. That's when experience matters; the times when all the years of training and knowledge come into play; the unexpected moments—no way to anticipate them—when what seems to be simple and ordinary is neither. That's when science can save a life.

Still, it's surprising how much of the time it doesn't really matter. The human body is an amazing organism whose natural state is health and wholeness. What we don't understand about it still exceeds what we do, yet somehow this essential fact never seems to prevent us from intervening: prescribing antibiotics that may or may not be necessary; operating on tiny tumors that may or may not ever kill us; the list is endless. We mustn't just stand there. We're expected to do something! Anything! And yet so often our patients get better not *because* of us, but *in spite* of us. So what else can we do but keep them company on their journey from sickness to health, perhaps making them laugh along the way. Truly, the art of medicine consists of amusing the patient while nature takes its course.

## SECOND LAW

# It is impossible to make an asymptomatic patient feel better.

**"I** FEEL FINE, DOC."

"Okay," I respond. "Then why are you here?"

"I'm just here because my wife/mother/husband/daughter insisted that I come."

"I see," I say, even though I don't. But I am a master of the patient interview. We doctors call it "eliciting a history." I am never at a loss for questions, even the ones that may seem obvious.

"Why did your wife/mother/husband/daughter want you to come in?"

"Well, I had this chest pain that used to come and go, but

not for a while now. My right knee has been sore ever since we got back from our hiking vacation in the mountains, and this spot on my arm used to itch, but it's fine now."

*I am a master of the patient interview*, I repeat to myself as I collect my thoughts. Which symptom to explore first? The correct answer is: the one that is bothering the patient the most.

Damn, I'm good at this!

"Which of these things is bothering you most?"

"None of them, Doctor. I feel fine."

The problem is that he really does.

Did Marcus Welby see healthy people? It seemed like everyone who walked into his suburban stone ranch house ended up with a definitive diagnosis, usually by the first commercial, however well they might have felt at the beginning of the episode. I think the main difference was that all of his patients had a script that said there was something wrong with them. In real life, people often feel just fine. But in those cases, what do I have to offer? How can I make them feel better? What's better than "fine"?

Of course, there are many medical conditions that cause no symptoms at all. People feel perfectly fine, sometimes until it's too late to do anything about a previously invisible and/or unknown problem. The mantra of "Early detection!" has permeated our popular culture until people believe that the only reason they ever got sick at all is that the illness wasn't caught soon enough.

People are also influenced by random events. Perhaps their neighbor two years younger has just had a massive heart attack, or their brother was recently diagnosed with diabetes, or they've just discovered that their hairdresser's mother-in-law has breast cancer. Whatever it may be, the fear that there's something wrong with them despite the fact that they feel fine is what drives them to me.

What these patients are really saying is "I'm worried." Even though they feel fine, a loved one has somehow managed to instill a sense of distress that can be relieved only with a visit to the doctor. My job is to relieve that fear, and I'm often damn good at that. Usually I just take a complete medical history and perform a physical examination. Sometimes I order a blood test or two, and perhaps an x-ray. At that point I can often tell patients there is nothing wrong with them. They feel fine, and they *are* fine. They shake my hand and clap me on the back, thanking me as they leave the office. Another job well done.

Damn, I'm good!

Of course there are other times when no amount of reassurance from me can assuage the patient's fear that something is dreadfully wrong.

"My great-aunt Sarah felt just fine, too, until she dropped dead of halitosis, Doctor. How can you be sure that's not what I have?"

Resisting the urge to explain that no one suffering from halitosis ever died of it (while realizing that the same cannot necessarily be said for such a patient's family and friends, and wondering if the patient understands that "halitosis" is just the medical term for bad breath), I probe further into the family history.

"How old was your great-aunt Sarah?" I might ask.

"Ninety-seven," comes the helpful answer. "But she felt just fine."

These are the people for whom "feeling fine" will never be good enough. Unfortunately, there is nothing I can do to help them.

And then there are the times when despite feeling perfectly fine, the patient is actually anything but. Then it falls on me to find a way to make him feel less fine. This is when it can get tricky.

When I find a too-high blood pressure, a dangerously high cholesterol level, or abnormal kidney or liver function on blood tests, or when I feel that little "thickening" during a breast exam, I know that although these people may feel fine, they aren't. If I don't do something—or, more correctly, if I don't convince them to do what I recommend—I know that the time will come, sooner or later, when they will not be feeling fine at all.

But how the hell am I supposed to motivate a patient who feels fine to do things that might in and of themselves make him feel less fine?

Medications have side effects:

"Fatigue, depression, bad dreams, and impotence? Are you kidding me, Doc? No way!"

Screening tests can be uncomfortable:

"Where, exactly, are you proposing to insert that into my body? *How* far? I don't think so!"

Modifying one's diet to eliminate beloved foods, and for what?

Patient: "I feel fine, Doc. What do you mean I have to give up eating sweets, breads, and pasta?"

Me: "Oh, and you should also limit your salt intake."

Patient: "But Doc—I feel fine!"

It's too bad that diseases like high blood pressure, diabetes, cancer, and kidney and liver failure often cause no symptoms in their early stages, which is ironically when treatment can often do the most good.

So I take a page from the book of the loved one who got the patient into the office in the first place. I predict the future. I paint a picture of illness yet to be. I describe in detail as precise, specific, and horrific as I can muster the terrors and torments that await. I generate fear; the more anxiety, the better. Then I offer relief: take this medication; get a colonoscopy or mammogram; avoid carbohydrates, exercise and lose weight. Only if they do as I say can they avoid the certain agony we describe, even though they feel fine—for now.

A PHONE CALL IN WINTER: "Doctor, my husband just came in from shoveling snow and says his chest feels heavy. He's all sweaty and he looks kind of gray to me," says the wife of a patient with diabetes and high blood pressure.

Well aware of this man's very high cardiac risk, I answer, "It sounds like he may be having a heart attack. I think you should take him to the hospital."

I hear murmuring in the background. Finally, the wife returns to the line.

"He says he doesn't want to do that."

"Okay," I respond cheerfully and with perfect equanimity. "Is his will up to date?"

A brief—very brief—moment of silence.

"I'm taking him to the hospital."

"Very good," I reply. "I'll meet you there."

THE HEART IS AN AMAZING, fist-sized lump of hollow muscle with sinews and flaps of tissue that convert its rhythmic pumping action into the one-way flow of life-sustaining blood. Like any other muscle, though, it also requires its own blood supply. Although the body's entire blood volume passes through it multiple times an hour, unless some of it gets into the heart muscle itself, it won't go on pumping for long. Fortunately, the heart gets first crack at the richest, reddest blood; the stuff with the greatest amount of oxygen.

After making a complete circuit of the body, the poor,

tired blood returns to the right side of the heart. It is dark maroon in color, having left all of its oxygen behind in the body's tissues. Its hemoglobin is loaded with the waste gas, carbon dioxide. The first chamber the blood enters, the right atrium, serves as a little fuel injection pump, giving the blood a kick into the larger pumping chamber. This chamber, the right ventricle, gives a firm squeeze and sends the blood squirting out into the lungs. As the blood ekes its way through the tiny capillaries in the walls of the alveolar air sacs, fresh oxygen moves through the thin walls, which are only one cell thick, and binds to the hemoglobin, brightening its color from a dusky maroon to a bright, vibrant red. Carbon dioxide diffuses away, across into the alveoli and up the bronchial tree, to be expired into the atmosphere, returning carbon to the plant kingdom for its metabolism. Invigorated with its renewed oxygen load, the blood returns to the left side of the heart.

This atrium is thicker, and squirts a brisk shot of blood into the left ventricle, the workhorse chamber of the heart. The ventricle gives a mighty squeeze and forces blood out into the biggest artery in the body, the aorta, with enough pressure to drive a column of mercury 120 millimeters into the air. At the base of the aorta lie three delicate leaves of tissue that slam shut, preventing the blood from sloshing back into the ventricle, as if to say, "Get out and *stay* out!" And just above these little leaflets of the aortic valve lie two little tiny holes: the entrance into the heart muscle itself.

These two tiny openings lead to two arteries that sit atop the heart like a crown, which is why they are known as the coronary arteries, as in "corona," Latin for "crown." They immediately begin dividing and plunging deep into the muscle tissue, delivering oxygen and nutrients to the cells of the heart even as it continues to beat.

But all is not always well in those tiny passageways. Deep within their dark recesses, cholesterol-laden plaques can build up. Still, the blood gets through. Blockages that do not obstruct flow cause no pain, no symptoms, nothing patients can notice while the blockage progresses. The patient feels just fine.

One day, however, something happens inside one of those narrowed blood vessels. It may be a tiny piece of cholesterol plaque that breaks off and flows downstream a little ways; just far enough for it to completely block the smaller vessel. Or maybe there's a microscopic tear in the lining that sets off the clotting cascade, the mechanism that works wonderfully to prevent bleeding to death from superficial wounds by converting liquid blood into a firm clot. But when activated internally, this wondrous chain reaction acts as a double-edged sword. Instead of staunching the flow of blood out of the body, it prevents the blood from reaching the beating muscle cells downstream. This is the patient who no longer feels fine.

It may present as a vague pressure in the chest that goes to your left arm or your jaw. It may become hard to breathe;

you may break out into a cold sweat, or even vomit. There can be an overwhelming fatigue, worse with activity, that can escalate over hours or days. Or a heart attack can hit you like a figurative ton of bricks. Imagine an invisible wrecking ball swinging down unseen and smashing you right in the heart. You clutch at your chest, clawing as you try to catch your breath while the life-giving pump of muscle dies; muscle cells bursting as, deprived of blood and oxygen, the pump fails. If a large enough section of heart muscle is knocked out, you won't survive to get to the hospital. Your wife or child or grandchild may come into the room to find you writhing on the ground as you gasp your last breaths. And right up until those final moments, you were feeling just fine.

I'LL NEVER FORGET the first time I ever heard a surgeon giggle. A patient of mine had gone to see this surgeon because the patient wanted a large fleshy lump removed from his back. The tumor was something called a lipoma. It was completely benign and would never threaten the patient's life, even though it would continue to slowly grow bigger. The surgeon sent the patient to me to make sure he was healthy enough to undergo the operation.

If you need an emergency operation, the amazing doctors who administer and monitor your anesthesia are pretty damn good about keeping you alive during the procedure. Surgery—even minor surgery like removing a large lipoma—always carries risks. The good doctors like to know about any organs functioning below peak capacity so they can compensate for your body's limitations. In an emergency they have little choice, but if the operation does not have to be performed before sunset (or sunrise, if it happens to be night; this has nothing to do with the time of day; it's the medical way of saying "it has to be done *now*"), the surgeons and anesthesiologists usually prefer to know that you won't die on them because of something that they didn't have to do to you. It was my job to make sure this guy was in good enough shape to tolerate the surgeon's meddling.

The first thing I did, as I usually do, was to take the patient's blood pressure. I wrapped a Velcro-covered plastic cuff around his upper arm, closed the valve above the rubber bulb in my hand, and began to pump. The idea is to inflate the cuff enough to cut off the blood flowing to his arm and then slowly release it while listening to the blood flow through an artery. I read the pressures by watching the column of mercury attached to the cuff.

The column of mercury goes up to 300 millimeters. Normal blood pressure is 120/80 or lower. High blood pressure is defined as above 140/90. But with this patient, I had to keep pumping and pumping and pumping. Every time I thought I had the cuff pumped up high enough, it wasn't. Just how high *was* his freaking blood pressure?

Finally I got the reading: 240/140. For good measure I repeated it on the other arm; it was the same.

Then I looked at his pre-admission blood test: his kidney function was reduced to only about 25 percent of normal.

No way was this man safe to go to surgery, especially for such a ridiculously trivial procedure. I called the surgeon, hoping he wouldn't be angry at me for cancelling the operation.

"Doctor? I'm calling about your lipoma patient."

"Yes? What about him?"

"Well, his blood pressure is 240 over 140, and his kidneys are three-quarters gone."

That's when the surgeon giggled.

"He's all yours," was all he said. "Let me know when he's ready."

The saddest thing about this particular patient is that he felt just fine, and that he had no idea what his real problems were. Even though his blood pressure made him a walking time bomb (heart or brain; place your bets as to which would go first), it turned out to be his kidneys that were failing and he had no clue. No one does when it's the kidneys.

THE KIDNEYS ARE A PAIR of bean-shaped organs tucked up under the back of the diaphragm, much higher than most people realize. Heavy with blood, the smooth brown surface beneath the capsule belies the complexity within. The renal arteries enter at right angles, then rapidly branch into smaller vessels, culminating in arterioles that supply the functional unit of the kidney: the nephron. The heart of each nephron is a microscopic tangle of tissue called the glomerulus that filters the body's entire blood volume multiple times a day.

This delicate mechanism is amazing. Functioning properly, it retains proteins, sugars, and other nutrients the body can ill afford to waste through indiscriminate excretion. But as always, with great delicacy comes great fragility. Poisoned by the metabolic derangements of diabetes or damaged by the pounding of too-high blood pressure, or even just as the kidney ages, the glomerulus hardens and fails, its blood supply shunted away to other functioning nephrons. Once a nephron goes, it is gone for good. Fortunately, the kidney is a prime example of the splendid redundancy of the human body: the one million nephrons present at birth are significantly more than necessary to filter enough blood to sustain life, even as their number decreases slowly but steadily with age.

The deterioration and disappearance of nephrons doesn't hurt a bit. But as your failing kidneys no longer filter enough waste from your blood, poisons build up. Eventually, a waste product called urea can settle on your skin like a fine frost. Without enough nephrons to siphon potassium, another waste product, out of the bloodstream, its level in your blood may rise dangerously high. If the potassium goes high enough, it can disrupt the flow of ions in and out of the cells that pace your heart and keep it beating. This is the how lethal injection works when prisons use it in carrying out the death penalty: raise the potassium and stop the heart.

It works.

In this modern day and age, though, there are treatments for failing kidneys: machines that perform many of the kidneys' excretory functions through a process known as dialysis. The miracle of a semipermeable membrane—a film that allows water and small molecules to flow across it in one direction only—is harnessed to function as an artificial kidney. Blood from the body flows across one side of the membrane while solutions with carefully controlled concentrations of physiologic solutes hide coyly on the other side. Wastes cross the barrier, out of the blood and into the machine, to be flushed away almost the way nature intended.

But how does the blood get from the body to the machine? The devilish details of dialysis are in the mechanics.

There are generally needles involved; large-bore ones, the better to carry greater quantities of blood so that your thrice-weekly hemodialysis treatments can be completed within a reasonable time frame. At least two needles are required to establish a full circuit: blood runs out of the body, into the machine where the magic occurs, and then back into the body. To make it easier, a surgeon can create an artificial connection called a fistula between an artery and a vein in your arm, producing a big fat ropy lump to serve as a receptacle for the needles to plug directly into your bloodstream. As the fistula purrs with the thrill of arterial pulsation, it also serves as a constant visual badge of your unenvied new membership in the cadre of dialysis patients.

Three times a week you report to your station, settle yourself into a vinyl recliner, and await the needle nurse who plugs you into your machine. For three hours—or more; some physicians believe American dialysis patients have higher mortality rates than their compatriots in other countries because Americans use shorter dialysis sessions—you sit, tethered to the artificial version of an organ the rest of us carry under our backs. (At least you don't have to get up to pee. Your kidneys aren't working, remember? No kidney function means no appreciable urine output. Your bladder atrophies with disuse; the tissues lining it become thin, bleeding easily. But no matter; you're not using it.) Three hours to kill. There's almost always a television blaring somewhere, if you care to watch. Many people nap, exhausted by the toxic effects of the poisons built up in their bodies. Three hours a day; three days a week; every week. No stoppages; no breaks; no vacations, unless you can locate a dialysis center at your destination that has room for you and is willing to dialyze you during your stay. Week in and week out. Three days a week. Three hours a day.

Even when you're not physically tethered to your artificial kidney, its reality permeates every moment of your life. Your diet is severely restricted. You are forbidden to consume more protein, salt, or water than can be removed through dialysis; otherwise, it accumulates and you swell with fluid, raising your blood pressure even further and putting more and more of a strain on your heart.

Three hours a day; three days a week; every week; week in and week out.

You don't have to do this. You can eat and drink what you want, sleep late, and not bother with dialysis. But you won't feel fine for long. In fact, you'll die within about a week.

IT TURNS OUT that a lot of people have interesting definitions of "feeling fine."

"I'm afraid you have diabetes," I told a middle-aged man one day.

"Are you sure, Doc?"

"Yes, I am. Your blood sugar is over 200 milligrams per deciliter. Are you sure you're not having any symptoms?"

"Like what?"

"Frequent urination, extreme thirst, blurry vision, things like that."

"Well, yeah, sure, I've had all that for a couple of years now. But I feel fine."

The capability of humans to deny the experiences of their bodies is unsurpassed.

DIABETES IS A TERRIBLY misunderstood disease. It isn't caused by eating too much sugar, even though its definition is indeed "high sugar levels in the blood." When everything is working right, the pancreas releases exactly the right amount of insulin at exactly the right time so that the body can actually use it to do stuff like move and think. But some unfortunate people are born with a resistance to their own insulin. At first, their pancreas adapts and makes more of it. But eventually the pancreas poops out. When it can no longer make enough insulin, sugar levels in the blood rise; the result is called diabetes.

There are two things that can prevent this.

First, don't consume as much sugar. The more sugar you put in, the more insulin is needed to process it. Less sugar coming in means less strain on the poor organ. As it happens, "sugar" in this instance comes from carbohydrates. All that yummy bread, pasta, rice, cakes, and cookies are turned to pure sugar once digested. That's what makes them no-no's in a diabetic diet.

Second, exercise regularly. It turns out that sedentary bodies are more insulin-resistant. The more the body moves, the better it works.

So although you must be born with the gene for insulin resistance, you can still forestall the development of diabetes by limiting your carbohydrate intake and not becoming a couch potato. Maintaining an ideal weight is beneficial for many things, including diabetes prevention.

What is not well understood is how the high blood sugar in and of itself causes so many problems. For some reason, sugar in high concentrations is toxic to nerves. After decades of basting in sweet stuff, the body's electrical wiring is fried. Nerve cells that carry pain information back to the brain no longer function properly. Sometimes they send off signals at random, or they do not respond at all. Diabetic peripheral neuropathy consists of either numbness or exquisite pain; it is difficult to treat but impossible to cure.

Blood vessels are also damaged by sugar. It may be the high levels of cholesterol spilling out of the liver as it tries to process all that sugar, but it is clear that diabetic blood vessels narrow. Their walls thicken, reducing blood flow. And tissues that do not get enough blood eventually die.

The classic presentation of a diabetic ulcer is a non-painful sore on the foot. Because you can't feel it, you keep walking on it. Because the wound isn't getting the blood supply it needs to heal, it festers as tissue dies. Hopefully, by the time your toe falls off you'll notice a problem. But even by the time you get yourself to a doctor, your problems are just beginning. Depending on how compromised the blood supply is to the limb, you may not get away with just losing your toe. Not infrequently you'll lose all five of them with an amputation across the middle of your foot, a surgical finger in the dike designed to help you keep your leg. If that doesn't work, the next step is an amputation below the knee. With luck, the stump heals; if not, you'll lose the leg above the knee. And remember: you aren't any better off on the other side. You can easily wind up without a leg to stand on.

And yet diabetes is the ultimate lifestyle disease. Although the inborn metabolic defect of insulin resistance must be present to develop diabetes, if you are born with it you can delay or even prevent the disease by limiting the amount of glucose you ask your system to process in the first place. Regular exercise, a diet that's limited in simple sugars and carbohydrates, and careful attention to maintaining ideal body weight goes a long way toward tempering the stern decree of genetics. People who are able to accomplish those goals can maintain their blood sugars in the normal range indefinitely, and can continue to feel just fine.

A T FIRST GLANCE, the patient looked pregnant. This turned out not to be the case for two reasons. First, the birth date on the chart revealed that the patient was seventy-something. Second, the patient was a man.

His abdomen was enormous and perfectly round. Veins under the skin appeared to flow from his belly button like a wild mop of scraggly blue hair. But the rest of his body was withering away. His spindly arms and legs looked even more scrawny next to that enormous belly.

I was a medical student on rounds at the Veterans Administration hospital, and this was the first patient assigned to me. The intern marched a group of brand-new third-year medical students into the man's room and pointed to the patient's abdomen.

"You're going to drain that."

"Drain what?" I asked. At least I think it was me. It may have been one of my classmates. We were all equally mesmerized at the sight of the patient's distended belly. Years of alcohol consumption had finally destroyed his liver. Instead of processing nutrients and detoxifying poisons, the organ had become nothing but a lump of hard gray tissue that couldn't even produce enough albumin to keep fluid in his blood vessels where it belonged. Now the fluid leaked continually into his abdomen, where it accumulated to monstrous proportions.

The intern opened a sterile pack of instruments and showed me how to put on rubber gloves while the other students looked on. I willed my hands not to tremble as I held a wicked-looking needle just inches away from the man's skin.

"Just stay in the midline, halfway between the umbilicus and the pubis," he directed.

I hesitated.

"What if I miss?"

Both he and the patient began laughing.

"Honey," the intern said, "it's like popping a beach ball. You're *not* going to miss."

Indeed, the procedure was as straightforward as he claimed. He connected a drainage bag to the catheter I inserted over the needle and we all watched as the clear, straw-colored fluid began to drain.

I saw one of my classmates nudge another.

"I wonder when we'll get a chance to do that," I heard him whisper. The intern heard him too, and laughed again.

"Don't worry. You can do it the next time."

"When will that be?" asked my classmate.

"A few days." Our collective jaws dropped. "The fluid will all re-accumulate by then. You can each do it while you're on rotation here."

The rotation lasted four weeks.

The patient, however, lasted only three.

THE LIVER IS THE LARGEST solid organ in the body. Nestled up under the diaphragm on the right side of the abdomen, the liver is the body's metabolic factory. Because one of its major functions is to protect the body from substances invading it via the mouth, the liver gets first crack at every drop of blood that receives absorbed nutrients from the gastrointestinal tract. The organ is remarkably homogenous. Each individual liver cell has all the metabolic capacities of the entire organ. Each one contains all the enzymes required to process nutrients, detoxify toxins, and produce assorted essential substances.

To the liver, anything that isn't a nutrient is a toxin. This includes all the drugs, vitamins, and herbal substitutes that people so painstakingly choose from shelves teeming with amber bottles; these substances, however, rarely do anything more than produce expensive urine.

Yet as robust as it is, the liver is vulnerable. Certain viruses are so prone to infecting the liver that they take their name from it: in medical terminology, any word that starts with hepat- or hepato- refers to the liver. Medicine has now discovered at least five different hepatitis viruses. And despite the liver's amazing regenerative capacity, some livers cannot endure a decades-long onslaught of alcohol, one of the most potent of all liver toxins. Any cells that do manage to regenerate will also perish as long as the poisoned environment remains. The cells die, leaving shrunken, nonfunctioning tissue where once there was a firm, vital organ. And once the disruption of normal liver tissue known as cirrhosis sets in, there is no more regeneration.

As your liver begins to fail, blood can no longer flow through the hardened tissue. Pressure quickly backs up into the GI tract. The path of least resistance leads to veins at the lower end of the esophagus that swell and dilate; the mechanism is identical to that of hemorrhoids formed in the rectum. Just like hemorrhoids, these dilated esophageal veins known as varices can bleed, except that the volume of blood is much greater. Once those varices let loose they may never stop, and you can easily bleed to death into your stomach.

Damaged liver cells no longer make proteins. Without albumin's oncotic pressure to hold fluid in your blood vessels, capillaries become leaky; fluid oozes out of the vessels, and your legs begin to swell. The skin stretches painfully as fluid seeps into the tissues, eventually breaking down into ulcers that continuously weep jaundiced yellow fluid.

Fluid also collects in the abdomen, as I discovered with that interesting first patient at the VA. By the time that process is established, there is no way to reverse it. Ammonia and other toxins build up in your blood and cloud your brain as you drift into a coma.

It isn't a bad way to die.


EARLY IN MY PRACTICE, one of my patients was a woman with pain in her back. I began taking the history as I always do, remaining friendly as I tried to establish rapport. When you think about it, we doctors can ask some pretty personal questions, so Marcus Welby, I, and other master interviewers try to ease our way into a relationship. After I had learned everything I needed to know about this woman's back, I asked, "Is there anything else bothering you?"

Apparently I hadn't warmed her up quite enough yet.

"Well," she said, "I have another problem, but I don't know if I want to tell you about it yet."

"That's fine," I said.

I changed the subject and asked about her past medical history, surgeries, allergies, and so forth. I was warm and charming, as always, and after about ten more minutes she announced that she was ready to confide in me.

"I've had a bad breast for about five years now."

Those were her exact words.

It was her left breast, and the only reason she was finally willing to bring it to someone's attention was that the seat belt in her car was starting to hurt when it pressed there.

She wasn't sure how the problem had begun; probably with a lump. But now the entire breast was hard, red, and shrunken. It was the first time I had seen a locally advanced breast cancer, and it was impressive. But aside from the slight discomfort when the breast was compressed, she felt fine. (Except for her back pain. Interestingly enough, that turned out not to be related to the cancer. She had back surgery and felt just fine—until she died from her breast cancer about seven years later.)

CELLS ARE REMARKABLE THINGS. Every one of us humans begins as a single cell—a fertilized egg—that starts dividing immediately. The cells quickly begin to differentiate, developing into specific types, then faithfully perform their fated functions throughout life. All cells use oxygen and glucose to generate energy for their metabolism, whatever their other tasks may be. Some divide and reproduce; others are more static. But there are times when something goes wrong with this carefully orchestrated mechanism.

Although it's not fully understood, the careful regulation that keeps cell growth in check occasionally fails. Instead of cheerfully performing only its assigned function, the cell begins to divide, over and over, spinning out of control and growing into a mass of unruly tissue that is unresponsive to the body's normal regulatory signals. As that mass grows ever bigger, pieces of malignant tissue may break off and float downstream through either blood vessels or lymph channels, growing into more masses of tissue wherever the pieces happen to lodge.

We call this cancer.

It doesn't hurt. Not at first. In the beginning, the tiny masses of cells can't be felt; can't be sensed; can't be detected. You feel just fine. Sometimes there are early signs: blood in the urine from cancer of the bladder; a mole that grows and changes color, heralding malignant melanoma; vaginal bleeding after menopause from cancer of the uterus. But often—too often—there is nothing: a tiny lump in the breast that cannot be felt; a stomach cancer that feels just like a regular ulcer; a growth in the colon that causes no symptoms at all until it begins to obstruct the passage. While the cancer is still small enough to cut out completely, or burn away with radiation, or chemically eradicate with medication, you feel just fine.

But if you ignore it, or decide that it will eventually go away, or pretend that you didn't really notice anything, the cells will continue to divide and grow and invade and spread. You don't bother with that mammogram or colonoscopy; you pay no attention to that spotting of blood.

The tumors will continue to enlarge, destroying whatever tissues they invade. When they go to your skeleton, they will cause excruciating pain as the bones collapse with pathologic fractures. When they go to your liver, you will gradually lose the ability to detoxify poisons in your blood; as toxins build, you lose your appetite and begin to swell with fluid as you slip into liver failure. When they go to your lungs, you slowly suffocate as cancer tissue replaces the alveolar air sacs where oxygen is taken into the body. When they break through your skin, they form non-healing open wounds that smell like rotting meat. And when they go to your brain, they displace your thoughts, your dreams, your mind, everything you recognize as yourself, as you lose the ability first to think, then to move, and finally to sense anything around you.

By the time you're not feeling fine anymore, it will be way too late.

WHEN PEOPLE FEEL FINE, they don't have much motivation to do anything different: no reason to take medicine, no reason to exercise or to change their diet, no reason to get a mammogram or colonoscopy or blood test. So when I find something that I know poses a risk to a patient's health, I create alarm. By describing the natural history of the condition if it is left untreated, I can produce anxiety. Lots of it. As much as I need to. Because the only way for the patients to relieve this new symptom of anxiety is to do what I tell them to do. Because as long as

they're feeling fine, it is impossible to make an asymptomatic patient feel better.

# The urgency of the test is inversely proportional to the IQ of the insurance company pre-authorization clerk.

A TALE OF TWO PHONE CALLS:

Call #1: A young woman has a history of gradually increasing headaches, vomiting, and abnormalities on her neurological exam. These are symptoms of a brain tumor. The study of choice to rule out a brain tumor on this patient is an MRI of the brain. I know this because I am a family physician with four years of medical school education, three years of residency training, and the experience of more than a decade in clinical practice. I call the insurance company. For 40 minutes I explain to a seventh-grade dropout who is reading from a computer screen why it is important for this patient to have an MRI of the brain. For some obscure reason, the study is denied. Luckily, this particular company allows me the opportunity to speak directly to a physician if I wish, instead of to a seventh-grade dropout who is reading from a computer screen.

Do I wish? Indeed I do.

I am placed on hold for another 20 minutes, listening to oldies that are not so much golden as they are rusted. Finally the phone is picked up.

"Hello, Doctor?" I say.

"No, Doctor," comes the response from another non-doctor who sounds somewhat more intelligent than the previous person. This one's probably an eighth-grade dropout. "I'm sorry, but our medical director is unavailable at this time."

So what the hell am I supposed to do with my patient and the brain tumor I'm afraid she has? Before the actual words have a chance to spew from my incredulous mouth, she continues:

"Our policy in these cases is to go ahead and approve the study."

Huh?

"You mean that I have the right to talk to a doctor, but because the doctor isn't available to talk to me, you're going to just approve the test?"

"That's right."

Instead of trying to wrap my brain around the rationale behind this policy, I carefully write down the treasured pre-authorization number and then hang up, dumbfounded, realizing this has been an hour of my life I'm never going to get back. But at least my patient will get the appropriate medical care.

Call #2: A middle-aged man has pain in his knee. His knee hurts because he went jogging this weekend, now that the weather has finally warmed up, and he ran eight miles. No, he hasn't been running or doing any other kind of exercise over the winter. No, he didn't stretch before or after running. Why, yes, as it happens, he is about 40 pounds overweight. No, he hasn't tried putting some ice on the knee, resting it, or taking any medicine to help ease the pain. What he wants is an MRI of his knee.

I perform a physical examination and find that his knee is not red or swollen, nor does it hurt anywhere when I press on it. There is no fluid in the joint, and he is able to move it through its entire range of motion with only slight discomfort.

I explain to him that he has most likely sustained a mild strain of his knee that will resolve on its own with time and conservative therapy. He is not happy with my news. He again states that he needs an MRI.

What he really needs is a more rational initiation of an exercise program, some ice, a little rest, and some over-the-counter anti-inflammatory medicine. Cutting down on his caloric intake to lose some weight would also be helpful—though, granted, not immediately. There is nothing in his history or physical exam to suggest that there is anything seriously wrong with his knee; certainly nothing that would warrant an imaging study ahead of a trial of conservative care. I know this because I am still a family physician with four years of medical school education, three years of residency training, and more than a decade in clinical practice.

I decide to allow the pre-authorization process to serve its function. Surely not even an eighth-grade dropout would be allowed to approve an expensive MRI for such a trivial complaint.

But this time the pre-authorization clerk is a retired nurse. She is efficient and helpful, suggesting answers to the questions on her screen. So before I can say "defensive medicine," the test is approved and I have my pre-authorization number in hand—for an unnecessary study that I didn't want to order in the first place.

THE MOST IMPORTANT aspect of the practice of medicine is an accurate diagnosis. The most elaborate treatments, the most expensive medications, the most elegant surgeries are all for naught if the diagnosis is wrong. From time immemorial, the physician's primary diagnostic tools have been his senses and his intellect. Back in the days before Marcus Welby, medical diagnosis was almost entirely in the hands, eyes, and ears of the physician. Laboratory testing and diagnostic imaging are the products of modern times; the application of the advancement of science to the practice of medicine. Still, these wonderful new tools have their place.

The first step in diagnosis remains the medical history, which consists of the patient's experience of his illness: symptoms he may be suffering, their time course, exacerbating and relieving factors, and other things that the patient may or may not have realized were related to his primary complaint. I've always found it fascinating that even today, with all the elaborate equipment and testing we have available, the history is still the single most important factor in making a correct diagnosis. I can't count the times throughout my career—from my earliest days of patient care in medical school to the patient I saw yesterday—when a diagnostic puzzle was solved by taking more history.

Interviewing the patient is a critical skill; only its basics can be taught. The nuances of eliciting the relevant information from the patient—and often the family—take years to learn and decades to master. To this day, the skill of the diagnostician is reflected in the history he elicits. The patient begins with his chief complaint; after that, the interviewer's skill is knowing what other questions to ask, knowing what symptoms occur in association with others, and eliciting sometimes sensitive details from the patient. Marcus Welby, without doubt, was a master interviewer.

Obtaining an accurate history is not always an easy task. From the beginning of clinical training, we physicians are taught to begin the interview with open-ended questions. It can be frustrating when the patient provides similarly open-ended answers.

"How long have you had this problem?" I might ask.

"Oh, it's been a while," comes the all-too-frequent answer.

"Has it been days? Weeks? Months?" I ask, in a vain attempt at clarification.

"Oh, quite a while, I would say."

Let me try something a little different:

"Well, when did it start?"

"It began after we got back from vacation."

"And when were you on vacation?"

"Oh, it's been a while now."

While it can be difficult to pin down the details of the medical history, the general rule about listening to the patient without interruption remains the best advice. Many more times than not, the uninterrupted patient spontaneously provides all the details needed to make the diagnosis—although there are some patients who do go on for a while.

The next step is the laying on of hands: the physical examination. The techniques of inspection, auscultation, percussion, and palpation—looking, listening, tapping, and feeling—still taught to students today are the skills that stood their ancestors in good stead. One minor quibble is that although we learn the techniques, we are left to figure out on our own that we need to explain them to our patients. For example, when examining a painful limb or other area of the body, we are instructed to begin with an unaffected area. This allows us a basis for comparison, as well as to minimize discomfort to the patient. As our instructors put it, "Once you hurt them, they won't want you to touch them again." Wise words. Unfortunately, I learned the hard way that our patients never heard them.

I am examining a patient with an injured left knee. I begin, as taught, by palpating the right one.

"Uh, Doc," says the patient, "it's the other knee."

I've discovered that I need to explain that I was taught to start with the normal areas and go where it hurts last. If I don't explain, then the patient thinks either that I wasn't listening to him or that I'm an idiot.

The real reason for the physical exam is to confirm the diagnostic impressions gleaned from the history. It is incredibly rare to encounter something completely unexpected during the physical exam. Marcus Welby would say that if you did, your history wasn't good enough.

Over the decades, surprisingly little has changed about how the medical history is obtained and the performance of the physical examination. But because the numbers of the things we can treat and the ways we can treat them have mushroomed, the need for diagnostic precision has increased accordingly.

Back when pneumonia often meant a quick and easy death, it didn't matter which germ was causing the disease. Only when science developed antibiotic drugs that could kill the invading bacterial organisms without killing the patient did it become vital to determine exactly which pathogen was causing the illness. Clinical microbiology remains a vital subspecialty of medicine today, especially as microorganisms evolve and develop resistance to the drugs we use to poison them, necessitating the development of ever more powerful drugs.

Chest pain with exertion—the pain of heart muscle not getting enough blood when blocked arteries are unable to supply the increased demand of activity—is called angina. When the only remedy we had was nitroglycerin, it didn't particularly matter which arteries were blocked. The patient's heart needed blood, and nitroglycerin caused the blood vessels to relax, relieving the patient's pain as it restored blood flow to the oxygen-starved muscle. We now have the capability to intervene and bypass those blockages, both in the operating room with coronary artery bypass surgery and in the catheterization lab, where tiny tubes are threaded through the narrowest openings to ream out the obstructions and support the vessel from within. Once you are able to intervene, you need a road map to describe the anatomy before you can begin the journey. Those road maps are produced with x-rays and other forms of diagnostic imaging.

IT WAS IN 1895 that Wilhelm Roentgen discovered the mysterious rays that could penetrate human flesh. Passing unseen and unfelt through the body, they could be completely blocked only by lead and other dense metals. Like other kinds of radiation, these so-called x-rays could form images on photographic film. Doctors quickly learned to correlate these images with abnormalities inside the body. Over the decades, this key event blossomed into the modern medical discipline of diagnostic imaging.

The earliest challenge was finding a way to differentiate between shades of gray on a standard x-ray picture. Varying densities of body tissues make bones show up white and air appear black. Everything else is somewhere between the two. It didn't take long to discover materials that blocked x-rays, therefore appearing white on film, and could also be ingested or injected. Barium sulfate—a chalky, insoluble white powder—could be used to outline the gut. Iodine-containing compounds were also found to be radiopaque. Any organ into which you could inject them would light up like a flare, producing bright white images in silhouette.

As fabulous as those pictures could be, the early diagnostic imagers weren't satisfied. They experimented with x-ray cameras and film and discovered that more detailed pictures emerged when they moved things around. Rotating the camera-film axis around the patient, a technique called tomography, produced beautifully detailed images. Once the digital computer made an appearance, diagnostic imaging exploded. Computerized tomography (CT scanning) shows the entire three-dimensional structure of every structure in the body.

CT still has its limitations, though. It's not very good for looking at structures protected by thick bone, namely the brain and the organs contained within the pelvis. Thus, more advances were to come.

Every molecule of water in the body acts like a tiny magnet. If you slide yourself into a tube containing a very strong magnetic field, all of those water molecules line up like tiny molecular iron filings. Send a radio wave into the field and it tips each of those little water magnets a little bit off its axis. When the radio wave stops, the molecules snap back into line with the external magnetic field again, giving off their own tiny little radio signal in turn. Connect a whole bunch of detectors to the outside of the tube, and connect those detectors to a whole bunch of really powerful computers, and you can create unbelievably detailed pictures by the process now known as magnetic resonance imaging (MRI).

For those patients who get too claustrophobic to spend an hour or more remaining completely motionless in the tight quarters of an MRI tube, and for other situations where radiation itself is harmful, there are still more diagnostic imaging modalities.

Taking a lesson from the bats and the dolphins, we learned that high-pitched sound waves sent into the body will "bounce back" to machines that create pictures from the echoes. Solid stones in gallbladders or kidneys show up bright white. Hollow, fluid-filled structures such as bladders and breast cysts are black, making ultrasound the perfect way to characterize assorted lumps and bumps. A hollow structure, for example, is almost never cancer; if it's solid, it needs closer examination.

Ultrasound is the perfect way to look at the unborn child, because it is impossible for the sound waves to damage tissue. Watching the heart beat eight weeks after conception, seven months before birth, drives home the reality of parenthood more powerfully than ever before possible. Monitoring the baby's developing organs allows for earlier intervention, often before birth—not to mention satisfying the near-universal impatience to answer the question "Boy or girl?" as soon as possible. Luckily, the technology remains less than perfect—or is it the purview of the bashful fetus?—so that gender surprises can still occur. Fortunately, bringing a little boy home to a pink nursery is not a life-threatening outcome.

Ultrasound can also be used to watch blood as it flows through arteries, veins, and organs. The Doppler effect, the reason that train whistles sound different if the train is moving toward you or away from you, is a property of sound waves. Using ultrasound waves in real time allows you to see not only moving tissues such as the heart and its internal structures, but also the speed and direction of blood flow. The ability of ultrasound to detect leaky valves, holes in the heart, and blockages in large blood vessels has transformed the field of vascular surgery into high-tech plumbing.

S O WHAT'S INVOLVED in actually obtaining diagnostic imaging studies?

"I want you to get a chest x-ray."

"What do I have to do, Doctor?"

"They'll just point a machine that looks like a camera at your chest, ask you to hold your breath, and take the picture. You won't feel a thing."

"Okay, Doc."

That was easy. Let's try something else:

"I want you to have an ultrasound."

"What do I have to do, Doctor?"

"Drink eight glasses of water, don't pee, then lie down on a table while a technician runs a microphone over your belly."

"After drinking eight glasses of water and not peeing?"

"Yes."

"Is this really necessary, Doc?"

"Well, it's the best way to see what's going on in your lower abdomen without using ionizing radiation." I've found that even without explaining in detail precisely why ionizing radiation is a bad thing, it just sounds like something to be avoided.

"Okay, you're the doctor."

That wasn't so bad. Let's take it one more step.

"You need a CT scan."

"What do I have to do, Doctor?"

"A few hours before the test is scheduled you have to drink at least two quart bottles of barium. It's a thick white solution that tastes like chalk, but you have to drink enough of it to go through your entire digestive tract so that your gut is visible on the films. Then you lie down on a table that moves back and forth through a huge metal doughnut that holds the cameras that whirl around you in a circle to take the pictures. You'll have to hold your breath for a few seconds when the technician tells you to. Then you'll get an injection of dye into your vein that will make you feel hot and flushed for a few seconds, though some people get nauseated and some may vomit."

"That's it?" gasps the patient.

"Sorry, there's more. I forgot to mention that if you have asthma you have to take Benadryl and a steroid pre-medication starting 13 hours beforehand. It might upset your stomach and make it hard to sleep. Oh, and we have to check your kidney function first just to make sure you won't go into kidney failure from the dye. And after the study is over you'll have to make sure to drink plenty of liquids and take a bunch of laxatives for good measure, just to make absolutely certain that all of the barium gets out of your intestine. If it stays in there too long, the colon absorbs the water and it gets as hard as a brick. You definitely don't want that to happen, do you?"

At this point, the patient is finding it hard to speak.

"It's very important that you have this study, though," I continue. "We have to make sure you don't have something like cancer."

The patient chokes out the magic words, "Okay, Doctor."

That took a little more work. Let's try this:

"We need to do an MRI."

"What do I have to do, Doctor?"

"You lie down on a table that slides into a tube just barely big enough to hold you, kind of like a round coffin, only smaller. Then you just have to lie absolutely still for at least an hour while the machines around the tube make deafening crashing noises as the machine gathers the information to create the images. We can give you some headphones with music to try and drown out the noise. If you move even the tiniest bit, then we won't be able to tell anything from the pictures, the study will be useless, and we have to start it all over."

"Do I need any kind of contrast injection?"

"Oh, yes. Sorry, I forgot to mention that. The injection isn't the same as CT dye, though, so you probably won't vomit."

"Is this test really necessary, Doc?"

"Only if you want to be 100 percent sure you don't have a brain tumor."

The patient gulps.

"Okay, Doctor."

I DON'T REALLY TALK to patients like that. Then again, they almost never ask me if a test is really necessary; my patients know that I don't order tests if they're not. The problem comes from patients who have made the decision themselves that they want a certain test. This is when I have to explain to them that there is a dark side to x-rays.

Some atoms have nuclei that are unstable. This phenomenon, known as radioactivity, occurs when the nucleus—the cluster of protons and neutrons in the center of the atom— suddenly ejects small pieces of itself into the space around it. Depending on how big these pieces are, how fast they're moving, and their proximity to other atoms, they can fly around knocking off pieces of other atoms' nuclei. If one of those atoms happens to be part of a molecule in a living cell, perhaps one of some importance to the cell—say, its DNA—suffice it to say that this is not a good thing. The cell needs its DNA in order to function properly. Without enough intact DNA, the cell dies. If the DNA damage happens to involve certain genes that regulate the growth of the cell, it is possible for the cell to begin growing abnormally; sometimes not stopping when it should. This is the cellular mechanism of cancer.

Radiation dose is the key factor. Large amounts of radiation bombarding many cells over short periods of time can cause burns and irritation; it is over the long term that they can cause cancer. Radioactivity was first described in 1910 by Marie Curie, and it eventually killed her and several other early radiologists and their assistants. Human cells can repair damage from small quantities of radiation. They have to; the greatest source of human radiation exposure is the sun. But the damage is cumulative, which is why cancer is more common later in life.

The doses of radiation that are used to take the pictures used in medical imaging are minuscule but still play a role in cumulative cell damage. This is one reason used in explaining to patients why they don't really need that scan "just to be sure," or why an x-ray "just in case" isn't really a good idea. If it's a trade-off between the patients' peace of mind now and cancer later, many can be convinced to deal with the uncertainty.

Sometimes I have the opposite problem.

"Mrs. Smith, we need to get an x-ray of your wrist."

"But Doctor, x-rays cause cancer!"

"Mrs. Smith, the human wrist is not supposed to be at an angle like that." I point to her wrist, which she is holding protectively in her other hand. "I'm pretty sure your wrist is broken, and we have to know how badly so the orthopedist can decide how best to treat it."

"But Doctor, I don't want to get cancer."

"One x-ray won't give you cancer, Mrs. Smith."

"Are you sure?"

"Yes."

"So if I get this x-ray, you can promise me that I won't get cancer?"

It's amazing I still have as much hair as I do, given how often I feel like pulling it out.

"I can't promise that you'll never get cancer, Mrs. Smith, but you really need this x-ray if you want the orthopedist to help stop your wrist from hurting."

This appears to be the winning argument.

"Okay, Doctor."


WITH ALL THE POTENTIAL hazards of diagnostic imaging, you might think that the exercise of pre-authorization began as a way to protect the poor, vulnerable patients from callous doctors determined to order every possible test, regardless of the medical need. And you might be right, but only if you also believed there really are little green men on Mars. In fact, the pre-authorization process arose in the late 1980s as a means of cost control.

Unfortunately, there's no getting around the fact that technology costs money. X-ray machines need film and cassettes to hold the film in place during the studies; chemicals to develop the pictures; assorted contrast media for different kinds of studies. Ultrasound machines need watery gel to improve conduction of the sound waves between microphone and skin, plus little electric bottle warmers to warm the gel, protecting patients' warm skin. MRI machines need all kinds of special non-metallic equipment for safe use in the immediate vicinity of a giant magnet. And then, of course, there are computers, computers, and more computers for everything from processing the images to registering patients. It adds up to a sizable chunk of cash, without even taking into account the salaries for the technicians who work all the machines that obtain the actual images and the professional fees for the radiologists who interpret them.

One might predict from the principles of economics that over time, diagnostic imaging costs should drop. CT scanners and MRI machines are indeed hideously expensive, but once the initial cost is recouped, the unit price per study ought to decrease. With increasing computerization and electronic image storage, even costs for physical film are disappearing. So why are the prices not going down?

"Doctor, my knee is bothering me. Can I get an MRI?"

"Mr. Jones, you're 75 years old and your knee has been hurting for 15 years. It's probably arthritis, and a plain x-ray is good enough to tell us everything we need to know."

"But Doc, can't you see many more things with an MRI?"

"Well, yes, Mr. Jones, but not the sort of things that are likely to be wrong with your knee."

"Look, Doc; I used to drive a crummy beat-up old Chevy with holes in the floorboards and a busted radio. Now I drive a brand-new Cadillac with all-leather interior, sun roof, heated seats, and a dozen-CD player. So tell me this: why should I settle for a boring old test like an x-ray when I can have a brand-new better one like an MRI?"

"Because medicine is not the same as cars, Mr. Jones.

When it comes to diagnostic imaging, newer does not mean better."

"Sure it does!"

And therein lies the rub. The American way is to covet the most recent. Newer, bigger, shinier, more beeping noises and flashing lights. There are a lot of buttons on an MRI machine. How could it not be better?

Even as patients are pushing for more expensive tests, the radiologists who, coincidentally, profit by providing them seem to be in cahoots.

A phone call to my local hospital's Department of Diagnostic Imaging:

"Hello, Dr. Isotope. I'm calling about my patient's chest CT. I got your report and I'm not quite clear about what it means."

"Let me see here. It says, 'If clinical concern persists, consider MRI.' Why isn't that clear?"

"Well, this patient originally came to see me last month with cough and a fever, so I got a chest x-ray that showed pneumonia. I treated her with antibiotics, but your report read that she should have another x-ray in a month to make sure the pneumonia had cleared. I sent her for that last week, but the report said that it needed to be compared to previous films. So I called your department back and asked them to please do the comparison. Then I got your addendum report comparing the new film to the old film, and it said, 'Recommend CT for completeness.' So I sent her for the CT, and now you're saying that I should consider MRI. Could you please tell me why?"

Dr. Isotope is clearly a very busy man.

"Look, Doctor, I'm not telling you how to practice. The report simply means that if you are still concerned about this patient, we can do an MRI to further evaluate any pathology in the chest."

"So what do I tell the patient?"

"Tell her she can call to schedule the MRI at her convenience."

"But does she need it?"

"That's up to you."

In a manner of speaking, it is indeed up to me. But when I am holding a piece of paper in my hand, signed by a radiologist, that says, "Consider MRI" and I choose not to order an MRI, I had better be damned certain that lack of an MRI isn't going to come back and bite me some day in a court of law.

Radiology—or "diagnostic imaging"—is an interesting medical specialty. At its core, the physician's task is to observe images of various types and render a professional opinion on their content. The more clinical information with which he is provided, the more accurate an assessment he can make of the images before him. When we send patients for diagnostic imaging, we are asking the radiologist to give us an opinion even if we look at the films ourselves. And like any other consultants, they charge for their services; as do all physicians, including Marcus Welby. The mortgage payments for that suburban stone ranch house had to come from somewhere. And so the cost of medical care increases with the rise of imaging technology.

## WHERE DOES IT STOP?

Left to its own devices, it probably wouldn't.

By the 1980s, certain medical insurance companies—and entrepreneurial physicians, among others—realized that they could insert themselves into the interaction between physicians and their patients and siphon off some of the money used to pay for these expensive new technologies. They never came out and said that's what they wanted to do, of course. Their marketing strategists called it "Managed Care."

Their claim was that rather than just collect the premiums from policy holders and pay medical claims submitted by physicians, they could somehow limit those costs by actively managing medical care. What exactly did this mean? Didn't Marcus Welby manage his patients' care? Of course he did, as does every other family physician in active practice, including me. It's what we do.

Managing medical care consists of deciding what tests are needed to diagnose a particular patient's ailment, and then making sure the patient gets them. Managing medical care involves referring patients to other doctors when a family doctor can't handle the problem alone. Managing medical care means reviewing letters from consultant physicians, noting when they recommend tests or procedures that have already been done or might be dangerous for that particular patient, or when they prescribe medications that either duplicate or conflict with those the patient is already taking. Managing medical care includes preventive care; keeping up-to-date with the latest recommendations for screening tests for asymptomatic patients, educating patients about the advantages of early detection and treatment afforded by the results of those screening tests, performing the tests or arranging for them to be performed, and explaining the results to the patient. Managing medical care certainly includes encouraging patients to adopt healthy behaviors and habits while avoiding those that are harmful. Managing medical care is called "practicing medicine."

So "Managed Care" instituted the pre-authorization process, supposedly to save money.

The underlying assumption was insulting: the implication that doctors were ordering unnecessary studies. In response to this "problem," the companies created "guidelines" for medical practice—ostensibly with input from practicing doctors, though in reality the guidelines were mainly based on recommendations from academic physicians and other researchers. If my patient didn't meet all the criteria for a test or procedure, the Managed Care company denied it. In point of fact, all the companies did was refuse to pay for it, but this is a distinction without a difference to most patients. Some don't have the money in the first place, and most of those who do refuse to part with it; after all, isn't their insurance supposed to pay for these things?

OVER THE YEARS, pre-authorization has become a game. If I can come up with the right answers to their questions, I win! Actually, my patients win by getting the tests they need. I will admit, though, that it took a few years to learn some of the tricks of the trade.

A call for pre-authorization begins with the basics. After navigating an automated menu for several steps, we finally encounter a human being whose first order of business is to ascertain that this particular insurance company actually has a responsibility to this particular patient.

Patient's name ("Please spell that"), date of birth, and insurance ID number are usually sufficient.

Office address, phone and fax numbers. Check.

"What facility will the patient be going to?"

This is where it gets tricky. Hospitals and other imaging facilities won't allow the patient to make an appointment for the study without having already obtained the pre-authorization. But in order to pre-authorize it, the insurance company will state that they need to know where and when it will be done. It's a perfect catch-22. We get around this by picking a date one or two days in the future and by agreeing with the patient ahead of time that he will go to a particular facility. Only then does the pre-authorization clerk get into the clinical details.

"What study is being requested?"

"A nuclear stress test. The patient had an abnormal treadmill stress test, so now we need to repeat it with nuclear imaging."

"What is the indication for the study?"

"The treadmill stress test was abnormal."

"Has the patient already had a treadmill stress test?"

"Yes."

"What were the results?"

"It was abnormal."

"Does the patient have risk factors for heart disease?"

"Yes, he has high blood pressure and diabetes, and he smokes."

"Does the patient have high blood pressure?"

"Yes."

"Does the patient have diabetes?"

"Yes."

"Does the patient smoke cigarettes?"

"Yes."

At seemingly random intervals throughout the clinical questions, requests to spell the patient's name and provide his date of birth and ID number are repeated.

"Has the patient seen a cardiologist?"

"No. I tried to make an appointment for him, but the cardiologist wanted to see the nuclear stress test first."

Silence on the line, except for the muted clicking of a computer keyboard. Finally, the magic words:

"Thank you for calling the pre-authorization center. This study has been approved. Please provide the patient with the following 25-digit certification number. Please be advised that this pre-approval is not a guarantee of payment. Payment is dependent on the individual terms of the member's plan, subject to limitations and exclusions of coverage in effect on the date of service."

I often find myself wondering how Marcus Welby would have handled pre-authorization.

Luckily, this particular patient's test was not terribly urgent. This likely explains the relative ease with which I managed to negotiate the pre-authorization process— because it is clear that the urgency of the test is inversely proportional to the intelligence of the pre-authorization clerk.

## FOURTH LAW

---

# There is no cure for Stupid.

S TUPID IS NOT the opposite of "smart." It is not a synonym for "ignorant," or for "uneducated." Stupid is worse, because it is intentional. And there is no cure for it.

There is no shame in not knowing. Information can be discovered; concepts can be learned. All that is required is a willing learner who knows there is something he does not know. It is the arrogance of ignorance—pride in one's lack of knowledge—that is as unforgivable in the physician as it is in the patient.

I WAS TAKING A HISTORY on a new patient, a young woman with no specific complaints.

"Have you had any medical problems in the past?" I asked.

"Oh, yes, Doctor. I've had terrible trouble with gall-stones and liver stones."

I looked up from my charting, puzzled. Gallstones are collections of precipitated pigments, bile acids, and choles-terol that collect in the gallbladder, an organ that dangles beneath the liver like a large green plum. Its function is to collect bile, a substance created in the liver, and to store it until it is needed in the intestine to aid in the digestion of fat. Gallstones are true stones, usually too hard to cut with a knife. They sink in water, and they are stable at room temperature.

There are no such things as "liver stones." I had to come up with a tactful way to inquire about them.

"What kinds of problems have you had with stones?"

"I had this friend who told me that most people have all these stones in their liver and gallbladder, and that if they aren't removed regularly they can lead to cancer, colitis, Alzheimer's, and all kinds of other things. She showed me how to do this thing called a liver flush. You mix Epsom salts in water and drink two glasses of it, once at 6:00 P.M. and once at 8:00 P.M. Then at 10:00 P.M. you drink one-half cup of olive oil and three-quarters of a cup of grapefruit juice within five minutes. Then you have to lie flat on your back immediately and not move for one hour. In the morn-ing when you go to the bathroom, you'll see all these green and tan stones floating in the toilet bowl."

"Huh?"

"Yes! It's the stones from your liver and your gallbladder. You can fish them out of the water and cut them in half. The centers look like green crystal. But if you want them to keep you have to refrigerate them, otherwise they melt."

"How big are they?"

"They can be the size of a quarter. Up to about an inch in diameter!"

I was dumbfounded. There is no way that any kind of stone can form in the liver. And there is no way for a one-inch gallstone, much less a whole toilet bowl full of them, to traverse the entire gastrointestinal tract without causing an obstruction.

I turned to the Internet and quickly found the explanation. It turns out that mixing olive oil with acid—supplied by both the grapefruit juice and the stomach—combined with the magnesium sulfate from the Epsom salts and potassium from the fruit juice produces globules with the same chemical components as soap. They contain no cholesterol or bile acids. They do not sink in water and they are not stable at room temperature. If you analyze them chemically, you will find nothing more than the fatty acids from the olive oil, acid from the grapefruit juice, and magnesium from the Epsom salts that you drank. They are not stones at all.

"See?" I said. "There's nothing wrong with your liver or gallbladder. Aren't you relieved?"

"But...but...I saw them! They're real! I don't believe

you. I have to keep doing those liver flushes at least once a week or all that stuff will build up in my system."

SEEING IS BELIEVING. It makes sense. If you spot a tiger in the brush, it is usually a better idea to start running away or girding for a fight than it is to stop and wonder if there's really a tiger there or if your eyes could be playing tricks on you. If you hear the rattle of an annoyed snake on the ground ahead of you, it probably makes sense to stop and look. Much of the input from our senses is intended to keep us safe in a hostile world, and yet it turns out that this built-in way of thinking leads us to many incorrect conclusions.

How can this be? Seeing is believing.

All we have to do is look up. The sun rises in the East and sets in the West; clearly the sun revolves around the Earth. There can be no doubt. We all see this with our own eyes every day of our lives, clear as crystal. How could it possibly be otherwise?

How many millennia of humanity did it take to realize that our eyes cannot always be trusted?

The role of science is to discover the truth beyond our eyes and to develop ways to work around the limitations of our brains. By developing telescopes and microscopes to measure things we can't even perceive, science is a way to understand the world objectively by getting out of our heads, as it were—to see things as they are, not as we might like them to be or as we may have been led to believe they are.

Everyone does not need to be a scientist, but it is important to understand that seeing cannot always lead to believing.

It turns out that deceiving the senses is childishly easy.

Think of optical illusions: figures that appear to be something that cannot be, but exist on paper. Steps that go ever upward, yet connect to where they began; leaves that are really fishes and vice versa. M.C. Escher was the master at creating images that could never be built in the three dimensions of the real world.

There is a style of painting known as trompe l'oeil—literally "fooling the eye"—which captures three-dimensional objects in a two-dimensional world so convincingly that the mind truly perceives it in three. I remember a painting that hung on the wall outside one of the largest lecture halls in my medical school. It was a tranquil beach scene of a deserted cove, inviting turquoise water and beige sand with lush tropical greenery in the background. But painted atop this scene, on the right side of the canvas, was the image of a telephone hanging on the wall. It was rendered in such lifelike, three-dimensional detail that more than once I found myself reaching for the receiver to make a call, only to have my fingers graze canvas instead of grasping the object my eyes told me was there.

"SO HOW HAVE YOU BEEN, ALICE?"

"I'm fine now, Doctor, but my back was awful a few months ago."

"Really? What did you do?"

"Well, I went to the chiropractor. He took some x-rays and showed me all the places the bones of my spine were out of alignment. Then he had me come in for adjustments three times a week and now I'm feeling ever so much better."

"Really?"

"Yes! Here are the x-rays he took before and after the treatments. He made me copies."

She pulls a pair of radiographs from the enormous bag at her side. Eyeing the bag, I have my own suspicions about the true source of her back pain. She thrusts the films at me and I dutifully hold them up to the light. Luckily, they reveal the "red-pencil" sign: the chiropractor has helpfully used a red wax pencil to mark the areas he feels are abnormal in the first film. Unfortunately, the structures he has circled are completely normal. I look at the second image and can see absolutely no difference between the two. I hand the films back to Alice as I struggle to keep my expression impassive.

"Isn't that great?" she gushes. "It was so bad before, and now you can see with your own eyes how much better it is. That chiropractor is like a magician!"

She is more right than she knows.


MAGIC IS ALWAYS SO EXCITING. The man (it's usually a man), mysterious and strange, introduces us to a world where the unreal seems to become real. He pulls the rabbit out of the empty hat. Where could it have come from? He pulls quarters out of your ear. They couldn't possibly have been in there already. He makes an elephant disappear. Where did it go? He saws a woman in half before our very eyes. How does he do it?

Even as we see these things, we know that the physical laws of the universe do not allow objects to be conjured out of nothing, or to disappear into thin air. We understand that the laws of reality that govern every other moment of our existence have not suddenly ceased to exist up on that magician's stage. The rabbit had to have been in the hat already. You may not have seen where the man in the black suit and fancy cape got those quarters from, but you have no doubt that they were *not* in your ear. We understand that there has to be a trick, and many of us delight in knowing how the trick was accomplished.

We make allowances for people who don't have the cognitive abilities to understand this. Children believe in magic, literally and concretely. As they grow older and their minds are able to grasp the abstract concept that their eyes can be fooled, they recognize that they don't have to re-think all the laws of nature just because they see something their minds know is impossible.

The Stupid is when adults with the presumed capability to understand the basic concepts of conservation of matter—things cannot appear and disappear at random—insist that something impossible is real. Even when shown how the trick is done, they cannot be cured.

A PATIENT NEEDS SURGERY FOR CANCER:
"Doctor, I'm so afraid. My grandmother died of cancer. It spread because they operated on it."

"What? Surgery doesn't cause cancer to spread."

"Yes it does, Doctor. She was fine before they opened her up. As soon as the air hit the cancer, it spread all over her and she was dead in three months."

"No, no. The cancer had already spread long before your grandmother's operation. They just didn't know it. She would have died at exactly the same time even if they hadn't operated."

"But they operated and she died."

"One thing may have happened before the other, but that doesn't mean the first thing caused the second."

"What are you saying, Doctor?"

"I'm telling you that the fact that she died after they operated does not mean that the surgery caused her death. Correlation and causation are not the same."

CAUSATION MEANS THAT one action makes another one occur. Every time the first action is taken, the subsequent one will result, and the subsequent action never occurs unless and until the first one has taken place. Slam the door and the windows will shudder. Yell at the dog and he will cower beneath the sofa. Other actions may yield the same result: the windows may shudder and the dog may cower during a thunderstorm. But causation means that the second action occurred specifically because another one happened first.

Correlation, on the other hand, simply means that two or more actions occur with a certain relationship to each other in time. One action may occur first and the other a certain amount of time later, or they may occur together. Sometimes the sequence can change. No other relationship between the actions is implied by correlation except the temporal one.

The baby smiles; the mother smiles back. The baby smiles again; the mother smiles again. The baby is learning that he can make his mother smile. He is learning that his actions have consequences. It is the same principle whereby he ought to expect to be grounded when he comes home past curfew 16 years later, though there are plenty of other lessons learned in between those two events. Still, from their earliest experiences, humans learn that they can affect their environment with their actions.

This is another cognitive trap.

In the context of interpersonal relationships, it is true that the behaviors of one individual do often correlate with the behaviors of others. Much of the time correlation and causation are indeed the same thing, be it smiling at an infant to make him smile, or bringing your wife flowers so she won't be mad at you for forgetting your anniversary.

It is also true that many observed physical phenomena correlate with—and cause—other actions to occur in the physical world. The lightning strike in an old, dying forest that ignites a conflagration; the prolonged rains that result in flooding and mudslides; no one is arguing the relationship of correlation and causation in these instances. Certainly a great deal of scientific enquiry proceeds because someone notices that certain events not previously thought to be related are in fact correlated in some way. Describing these correlations systematically and showing they can be replicated, preferably several times, is the essence of science.

But the human mind is hard-wired to believe that correlation and causation are the same in every instance. Things happen for a reason. Things *must* happen for a reason. This need is so deeply ingrained that we will seek out any correlation at all—no matter how far-fetched—to try to explain every event:

Lightning struck the barn because the son was late bringing the cows home the day before the storm.

The falling tree missed the house because Mother waxed the floor that morning.

The beautiful little girl up the street got leukemia because her mother had a caesarian section.

Our minds do not tolerate randomness. Understanding the phenomenon of coincidence—two separate events that have nothing to do with each other except their timing—is actually a very difficult concept.

Plausibility is an important factor in trying to determine

when correlation is in fact causation. It makes sense that rains cause flooding; both involve quantities of water. It may seem equally intuitive that lightning can cause fire, but in fact this requires an understanding of the nature of lightning. Lightning can be observed to set fire to an object it strikes, but in the absence of actually seeing it with one's own eyes, the concept of electricity and its relationship to fire is required to make the connection. Thus, the greater your knowledge within a given field—be it physics, geology, meteorology, or medicine—the better you are able to judge the plausibility of one given phenomenon being the cause of another. Still, it is an overwhelming temptation to attribute all kinds of relationships between events, however little you really know about the subject. This is the source of myths and old wives' tales: correlations that someone once thought made sense but, as the phenomena in question become better understood, turned out not only to be not correct but not even plausible.

"Magical thinking" is the term used to describe the insistence that a given correlation is causative, even when it cannot possibly be so. Children usually outgrow this by adolescence. Stupid never does.

THE PHONE RINGS. I roll over, wincing as I realize the clock reads 3:00 A.M.

"Hello, Doctor? I just got back from a business trip to India. Now I've been having terrible pains in my stomach for the last few hours, and I can't stop running to the bathroom."

Visions of strange parasites and tropical diseases begin coming to me, as I gather more information.

"How long were you there, and when did you get back?"

"I was there for a week, but we barely left the hotel. I got back three days ago, and I was feeling fine."

"What have you done since you've been back?"

"Yesterday I went to the health-food store to pick up some vitamins for my wife. I mentioned that I'd been away, and when the clerk found out I'd been in India, he told me I had parasites and I had to do a colon cleanse immediately or they'd spread through my whole body. I didn't want that to happen, of course, so I bought the stuff he told me to and followed all the directions. I took the pills before dinner and then drank a whole bottle of the liquid right before bed. Now my stomach is just killing me and I have the most awful diarrhea. It stinks, and it's this weird greenish color."

"Mr. Barnum, you didn't get parasites in India. If you stayed in the hotel the whole time and were there for only a week, and had no symptoms while you were there or for three days after you got back, there is no way you could have contracted any kind of parasite on your trip. None of that stuff from the health-food store was necessary. In fact, your symptoms only began after you took it. That's what's causing all your problems right now."

"What do you mean?"

"Those pills and liquids were probably just very strong laxatives that are now sending your intestines into spasm and producing the diarrhea."

"But the guy at the health-food store said I had parasites."

How much detail do I want to get into at 3:00 in the morning about my years of education, training, and experience in the study of medicine, and how they probably make me somewhat more qualified than a guy at a health-food store to advise Mr. Barnum about the causes and treatment of infectious diseases?

I sigh as my chances of getting back to sleep tonight fade into oblivion.

"You should be just fine in another couple of hours."

"But I'm supposed to take another dose in the morning. The guy at the health-food store said it was important to get all the parasites out."

"Well, Mr. Barnum, you have two choices. You can take my advice and stop ingesting dangerous substances to treat ailments you don't have that produce painful side effects like those you are experiencing right now, or you can do what the guy at the health-food store says and continue to suffer."

"But what about the parasites?"

"You don't have parasites."

"But the guy at the health-food store said I did."

Eventually, Mr. Barnum's cramping and diarrhea would resolve. The Stupid, however, is incurable.

I JUST DON'T GET IT.

I've had college science prerequisites, four years of medical school, three years of training, 20 years of practical experience in clinical medicine; and people still pay more attention to what their hairdresser, their cousin's brother-in-law who had surgery once, and the guy in the health-food store have to say about their health. And the rise of the Internet hasn't helped!

The quantity of information available on the Internet defies comprehension. That doesn't stop the determined patient from researching his every symptom and generating reams of results to bring along to his office visits. It's almost as if patients believe that if they search the Internet long enough, they can learn everything I know. While they can learn a great deal, being a doctor implies a great deal more—experience, of course; but the essence of a medical education is learning what to ignore.

Just as I don't worry about developmental milestones when the patient is 85 years old, I can safely ignore colon cancer screening in a teenager and prostate disease in a pregnant woman. The vast majority of information patients glean on the Internet does not apply to them, even when they think it does.

The Internet will tell patients who experience fatigue,

lightheadedness, and dizziness that their symptoms can be caused by heart attacks, anemia, depression, pregnancy, diabetes, myasthenia gravis, and an overactive thyroid gland. This is true, especially for generalized symptoms such as fatigue, but without the context of the patient's complete medical history and other associated symptoms—sometimes things the patient wasn't even aware were actually symptoms in the first place—there is no way that patient can come up with an accurate diagnosis. I don't mind patients researching their conditions on the Internet, but when they refuse to recognize the limitations of that research, things can get awkward.

In addition to valid medical information, the Internet also contains boundless quantities of medical nonsense. Some is innocent; some is pernicious distortion. Why do people continue to believe? Despite all the caveats about verification, it can still be difficult to evaluate information, especially when the person is unfamiliar with a particular topic. The biggest problem, though, is that people are terribly reluctant to change their minds about things they already believe. They may try to search the Internet for objective information, but they end up validating whatever is on their minds. If that patient with fatigue and weakness is afraid he has cancer, it isn't hard to find multitudes of web pages that associate fatigue and weakness with cancer. By the same token, he is also predisposed not to see the millions of web pages that describe all the other causes of fatigue and weakness. Even Marcus Welby would have had his hands full trying to reassure these kinds of patients; he's lucky he wasn't seeing people with access to the Internet.

Many patients whose information comes from questionable sources are easily reassured. When I take the time to explain that the web page they found is written by people who only want to sell them things—which is frequently the case—the usual response is one of relief. The printouts are pitched into the trash, and together we deal with the real issues.

The ultimate problem, though, is people who refuse to change their beliefs even when faced with incontrovertible scientific evidence to the contrary. These are the patients with implausible responses to every answer I try to give them. Like the child who flatly refuses to believe that the rabbit was already in the magician's hat or that the elephant didn't really disappear, or the guy at the health-food store who tells a patient he has parasites, they are incurable.

INTERVIEWING ANOTHER new patient:

"Are you taking any medicines on a regular basis?"

"Oh, yes. My naturopath prescribed a complete assortment of vitamins and supplements, and my homeopath has me on a regimen of herbal remedies. I see my chiropractor for regular adjustments, and I get acupuncture once a month. And I have an appointment with a Reiki healer, because the guy in the health-food store said she was really good."

"I see," I say, even though I don't. "Why do you do all this?"

"I believe in wellness!"

"Okay. I see it says here on your health questionnaire that you smoke a pack of cigarettes a day."

"Yes."

"And that you drink about a six-pack of beer every day?"

"More on weekends."

"How much exercise do you get?"

"I don't have any time."

"I'll bet the naturopath, homeopath, chiropractor, and acupuncture appointments take up a lot of it."

"Yes, indeed. But it's all worth it to me to be healthy!"

There is an imaginary spot on the wall in my exam room that is red and raw from where I imagine myself banging my head. There really is no cure for Stupid.

TECHNICALLY SPEAKING, there is no such thing as "alternative" medicine. Medical treatments proven by science to have a beneficial effect are called simply "medicine." All other treatments are divided between those that do not work and those that have not yet been shown to work.

Despite the protests of "alternative" practitioners, a great many of their treatments have in fact been proven not to work.

Homeopathy is a formulation of disease and treatment that developed before the modern understanding of chemistry. Mystical concepts such as "like cures like" and "the memory of water" result in outrageous assertions that a remedy becomes more potent the more it is diluted and the more it is shaken. No one with a third-grade understanding of science can possibly believe this. Yet it has a great following among the incurably Stupid.

Acupuncture claims to be based on ancient or traditional Chinese medicine. Mystical life energy, or "qi," flows through "meridians" running along the skin. Disease is caused by stagnation or blockage of this energy, which can be redirected or enhanced by inserting fine needles at specific points along the meridians. The more extensively and rigorously acupuncture is studied, though, the more it is revealed to be nothing more than an elaborate placebo. Sham acupuncture treatments using fake needles that do not penetrate the skin, although the patient perceives that they did, have been shown to have no more effect than using real needles. Inserting the needles at random sites instead of the actual "meridians" also has no effect on patients' perception of the results.

Chiropractors believe that misalignment of the spine causes disease. They claim to see these "subluxations" on x-rays, which they order liberally. Then they "adjust" the spine to relieve pain and other symptoms. They often prescribe multiple treatments, and even suggest "preventive" adjustments. Those who limit themselves to massage, heat, and other modalities of physical therapy are usually harmless, while others can be dangerous. Manipulation of the neck can cause strokes and spinal cord damage, for example. But the greater hazard of seeing a chiropractor comes when a medical condition goes unrecognized, undiagnosed, and untreated.

Reiki is one of many forms of "energy medicine." Rooted in vitalism, the concept of a "life force" that cannot be explained by the laws of physics and chemistry and cannot be detected by scientific instrumentation, it relies on a practitioner's ability to perceive "energy fields" and then somehow to effect change in their flow or other properties. It is by definition religious, requiring belief without objective proof. It's acupuncture without the needles.

The correct term for "alternative medicine" is "quackery," despite the many patients who continue to seek it out and the practitioners who continue to provide it.

Medical quacks have persisted through the eons, continuing to thrive by changing the language they use to refer to themselves and their treatments. "Holistic" became "alternative," which added "complementary" and then morphed into "integrative" medicine. "Natural," "organic," and "homeopathic" are words often bandied about in conjunction with all of the others. All of these terms have hijacked their dictionary definitions.

"Holistic" implies treating the "whole person." Although the term was coined in reaction to the fragmentation of specialty care, it has come to imply eschewing standard medical care; using herbs and other "natural" substances instead of pharmaceuticals; and emphasizing diet, exercise, relaxation, and meditation techniques in lieu of surgery and other medical treatments. Linguistically, it is a slap in the face to the family doctor. Marcus Welby provided "holistic" medicine. I provide "holistic" care. Family medicine is "holistic" by definition.

"Alternative" begs the question. "Alternative" to what? To scientifically proven, effective medical care?

"Complementary" implies that pseudoscience can add something to science.

The final linguistic incarnation of "quackery" is "integrative" medicine, another way of claiming that non-science-based therapies can exist side-by-side with medicine. Even as these practitioners try to claim the trappings of science, they refuse to acknowledge any studies that debunk their beliefs and they cling to non-scientific evidence such as testimonials. Testimonials, however, are about as useful as a roomful of people who saw the magician make the elephant disappear right before their eyes. They did indeed see it, but that doesn't mean it happened.

The only legitimate role for these faith-based therapies in the health-care setting is on the same footing as other religious modalities. Just as a hospital chaplain can be an important member of the medical team, I would have no problem with a Reiki or other "alternative" practitioner offering his services to patients in a medical setting. However, just as the chaplain understands that he or she is not providing medical care, the homeopaths and the Reiki healers need to understand that neither are they.

THE MAGICIAN SAWS the lady in half. Amazing! No blood, no guts, and her feet are wiggling the whole time. Then he puts her back together and she's none the worse for wear. Let's hear the applause!

Although some decry the breaking of the ancient magician's code of secrecy, there have been several books, websites, and television specials that give away the tricks; because, of course, it's just a trick.

The woman being sawed is limber enough to fit her body into the top half of the box. The bottom half is already occupied by a similarly limber second assistant, wearing the same shoes as the first, who sticks her feet out of the box at just the right moment to maintain the illusion that it's one woman inside the box, and who keeps wiggling her feet through the rest of the illusion. The rest is showmanship: the dramatic placing of the (fake) box ends; the sawing; the shrieking; the separation of the boxes to thunderous applause; then reversing the process as the applause crescendos again for the reassembled and now-intact assistant. Hurrah!

Once you know the trick, you can never look at it the same way again. Logic trumps magical thinking—in adults who choose to allow it. Yet somehow, when the trick involves medicine, the Stupid is incurable.

There is no shame in believing the evidence before your eyes. There is no shame in believing that correlation is causation because every time you wear your lucky baseball cap your team wins. There's nothing wrong with enjoying a good magic show, even if you never do figure out how it was done.

But for those who insist that energy fields, life forces, and liver flushes are real even when confronted with full explanations to the contrary, it is sad but true: there is no cure for Stupid.

## FIFTH LAW

# Bad things really do happen to good people.

I FIRST MET DENNIS when he was 33. He was a nice guy—a little overweight, a little high blood pressure, some sinus and allergy issues, but overall pretty healthy. Dennis was a middle manager who worked hard. He never smoked and rarely drank alcohol. He exercised as much as he could and tried to eat well. He and his wife were looking forward to starting a family.

About the same time I met Dennis I also met Mark. Mark was older, in his mid-fifties. He smoked and drank, hated to exercise, and loved nothing more than fast food; yet his blood pressure was perfect. So was his cholesterol, despite his terrible diet. He also refused to work. He had somehow been approved to receive Social Security Disability payments for an old back injury that had long since healed. He told me he knew he could work; he just didn't want to. He lived alone; he'd never married. There was no other way to put it: he was a miserable curmudgeon.

About a year later, during a ferocious blizzard, I got a heartrending call from Dennis. His wife had given birth to their first child three months early. The baby hadn't grown normally in the womb, so he was extremely small and very sick, hospitalized in a neonatal intensive care unit downtown. He wasn't expected to survive, and sure enough, about a month later, Dennis called to let me know the baby had died. Of course I was heartbroken for Dennis and his wife. I called them to offer my sympathies, then saw them later in the office, offering grief counseling as best I could.

Right around that time, Mark was having a flare of his chronic back pain. Nothing I offered was good enough: referrals for physical therapy, massage, over-the-counter pain medicines, a heating pad. Nothing would do except muscle relaxants and narcotic pain medicines, both highly addictive. At first I offered Mark small quantities of the pills, knowing that his pain was self-limited and would get better in time. He tried to browbeat me into ever larger prescriptions, but I stood my ground. Sometimes I wondered why he kept coming to see me. Frankly, I would have been thrilled if he had chosen to transfer his care to another doctor, but he never did. His back did get better and I eventually managed to wean him off all controlled substances.

Time passed. Dennis and his wife had two healthy little girls, and I rejoiced with them. Despite my continued efforts to get Mark to stop smoking and drinking, he never did.

A few years later, Dennis came to see me again. His dentist had discovered a white spot on the side of his tongue and was worried. I sent Dennis to an oral surgeon for a biopsy, which came back showing that the spot was cancer; a squamous cell carcinoma.

This was a shock. Dennis had no risk factors for cancer of the tongue; he didn't drink alcohol or smoke, especially pipes or cigars. There was simply no reason why a healthy man in his mid-thirties would develop this disease. But he had. After a series of imaging studies showed that the tumor hadn't spread beyond the tongue, the local ear, nose, and throat surgeons performed an operation called a hemiglossectomy on Dennis, which means they removed one-half of his tongue.

I saw him in the intensive care unit after the surgery. He was breathing through a tube inserted into a temporary hole cut in his neck. He was miserable. But he had his family, and his job, and a deep religious faith that got him through it. The tube was removed once the postoperative swelling in his mouth went down, and his tongue healed up beautifully. He quickly regained the ability to talk and eat normally. His prognosis was very good, because the cancer hadn't yet spread. As long as it didn't come back later some other place in the tongue—a local recurrence—he'd be fine.

The next day, Mark came to me complaining of a sore throat. I examined him and found that his throat was indeed red and sore, with white spots on the back of his throat and on his tonsils. I also found that the lymph nodes in his neck were swollen and hard. I wasn't too worried about them at that point, because swollen lymph nodes—also known as "swollen glands"—can occur as part of a sore throat; so I gave him a prescription for an antibiotic and told him to gargle with warm salt water to make his throat feel better and to come back in a few weeks. I wanted to make certain those swollen glands went down once the infection in his throat was treated.

Two weeks later Mark returned; his sore throat was all better. But when I examined his neck, those lymph nodes were still big and hard. They felt stuck to the tissues of his neck, and they didn't hurt. This worried me; hard, painless lymph node enlargement in the neck can be a sign of cancer somewhere inside the mouth or nose. And with all that smoking and drinking, Mark was at very high risk for those kinds of cancers. So I sent him off to the same ENT surgeons that were taking care of Dennis, and to no one's surprise they discovered that Mark had cancer of the throat.

Mark wasn't satisfied with the treatment options suggested by our local doctors, so he went downtown to one of the tertiary care centers for a second opinion. As it turned out, they recommended exactly the same course of action:

surgery followed by radiation. He went ahead with treatment at the downtown hospital, complaining all the while. Like Dennis, Mark had a temporary hole cut in his neck for a breathing tube. The doctors also inserted a tube directly into his stomach through his abdominal wall so that he could be fed without having to swallow. This was done because most people who have radiation after surgery for this kind of cancer develop severe inflammation of the mouth and throat; so much so that they can't eat and drink enough to stay alive. Mark had some discomfort, but his radiation treatments went extremely smoothly. He used the tube for some extra nutrition, but all things considered, he got through it quite easily. Not that you could tell by listening to him, though. He moaned and complained for weeks on end. I offered sympathy and what treatment I could to assuage the discomfort. Once again, nothing seemed good enough. It seemed like he enjoyed complaining, so I just let him. The radiation treatment was over in a few weeks and Mark's mouth and throat healed. Within six months the tube in his stomach was removed and Mark was back to normal.

Normal for him, that is: drinking like a fish and smoking like a chimney. Just about every other patient I've treated for cancer before and since has considered the diagnosis a wake-up call to make dramatic changes in lifestyle. Not Mark. No matter how much I tried to persuade, cajole, threaten, and convince, he wouldn't budge.

"I don't care," he said. "I have to die of something, so I may as well enjoy myself while I'm here."

"Why would you pick something as miserable as throat cancer to die of?" I asked.

"My throat cancer is cured!" he gloated. "I can't get that again."

"But you can! If you keep smoking those cigarettes and drinking all that booze, you can either get a recurrence of your original cancer, or even a completely new one."

"A new one?"

"Yes. It's called a second primary, and it means that another cancer has formed separately from the old one."

"Bah! I don't care."

There was no getting through to him.

Another year passed. I continued to see Dennis and his family for regular checkups. His daughters were growing beautifully, and I kept trying to get Dennis to lose some weight so his blood pressure would be easier to control.

Then one day Dennis came to see me after having seen his dentist.

"What's the matter?" I asked.

Dennis opened his mouth and stuck out his tongue. It looked perfectly normal to me. Then I suddenly remembered that Dennis had only half a tongue, which now so swollen that it was the size of a normal, intact tongue. The tumor had returned.

Now it was Dennis's turn to see the specialists downtown. The only thing they had to offer him was a massive surgical procedure, so complex it had to be conducted by two separate surgical teams. Surgical treatment of a cancer recurrence like this, when it's the only option left, is called "salvage surgery." One time, while looking over the reams of reports sent to me by the various specialists, my tired eyes left out a single letter and I read "savage" surgery. It was not inaccurate.

The surgeons' plan was to remove what was left of Dennis's tongue, including all the tissue in the base of his mouth inside the lower jaw, all the way to the chin. The floor of his mouth was to be rebuilt with a flap of skin and fat taken from his abdomen. This was known as a "free flap" because it would be completely severed from its original blood supply so that its artery and vein could be connected to the large blood vessels in the neck, the carotid artery and the internal jugular vein. To protect the flap, all of Dennis's teeth were pulled. He wouldn't need them; he would have no tongue and very few salivary glands, so he wouldn't be able to swallow. A tube was placed permanently into his stomach for nourishment. He also had a permanent trache-ostomy (a hole in his neck to breathe through), since the surgery at the back of his throat could block his airway.

The procedure took two teams of surgeons seven hours to complete.

By the time he got home Dennis was haggard. He'd been through hell, and he looked it. The inside of the bottom of his mouth looked like nothing I'd ever seen: no teeth; no tongue; just smooth, white, fleshy tissue that was actually skin from his abdomen. There were even small hairs growing out of it.

He couldn't speak, of course. Not only was his tongue missing, making enunciation impossible, but the permanent breathing tube in his neck didn't let air get up as far as his voice box. Even if he'd been able to form words with his mouth, he would have had to cover the opening of the tube with his finger in order to speak. He settled for writing notes, and took to carrying paper and pen with him at all times.

Within a week Dennis began spiking fevers. One of the incisions was infected with methicillin-resistant *Staphylococcus aureus*, a highly resistant germ he'd contracted in the hospital. Because no oral antibiotics were strong enough, he was re-admitted to the hospital downtown and given intravenous antibiotics. He came home again a few days later.

Not long after that, the surgeons discovered that Dennis had developed a blood clot in his internal jugular vein. Ordinarily it wouldn't have been a terribly serious complication, but in this case the blood supply to the grafted tissue in the floor of his mouth was at risk. If the flap lost its blood supply it could die and slough off, leaving Dennis with nothing but a raw, gaping wound inside his mouth. Once again he trekked downtown and was admitted. The medical team gave him blood thinners and watched the clot carefully; fortunately, the flap survived. Eventually, Dennis made it back home for good.

Meanwhile, Mark kept returning to the office for minor problems. They weren't minor to him, of course, but every little cold, cough, or sinus infection prompted a visit, and usually a demand for expensive antibiotics that were unlikely to do any good. But Mark was terribly insistent; after all, he'd had cancer.

"My immunity is down from all that radiation and chemo, Doc," he'd say. "You have to give me something to help fight this damn cold."

"If you'd stop smoking, Mark, you wouldn't get sick as often."

"How's that?"

"Every time you put a cigarette in your mouth, the chemicals in the smoke poison the cells that line your lungs," I'd answer. "You're making yourself sick."

"Just give me the damn drugs, Doc." He knew what he wanted and he refused to take "no" for an answer. Sometimes I gave them to him; most of the time I tried to stand my ground, hoping against hope he'd decide to find another doctor. I never did understand why he didn't.

Through it all, he followed up with his cancer doctors religiously. He followed their instructions scrupulously—all except the ones about quitting cigarettes and alcohol. His blood tests were always normal and his scans continued to show that he was free of tumor throughout his head and neck. He remained recurrence-free even as Dennis was struggling with each of his new obstacles.

Dennis's postoperative swelling took a long time to resolve, and even then it came back frequently. Any time Dennis caught a mild respiratory infection from one of his kids, he felt his throat swelling shut. Even though he had the breathing tube in his neck and couldn't suffocate, I gave him brief courses of steroids. These medicines reduced the swelling and made him more comfortable. He also got a lot of bronchial infections because his lower respiratory tract was no longer protected by the usual defenses provided by the nose and throat, as happens in everyone else. The tissues in his mouth contracted a bit—a normal part of healing—so eventually he was able to speak after a fashion. His wife and children understood him best. I tried, but he usually wearied of having to repeat himself and ended up writing me notes. He still carried pen and paper wherever he went.

And he couldn't eat.

The surgeons refused to let him try swallowing even liquids; the danger of aspirating food or fluid into his lungs was too great. Think for a moment just how much of our lives revolve around food; not just eating it, but planning meals, preparing them, and socializing with others in the course of consuming them. Dennis's weight was proof that he had always enjoyed this part of his life. And now it was gone forever. He pointed out to me that tossing a donut into a blender, liquefying it, drawing it up into a large syringe, and injecting it directly into his stomach just wasn't the same as eating it slowly, savoring it between sips of hot coffee. I couldn't even begin to imagine life without eating food, yet he was living it.

Amazingly, a testament to his will power and work ethic, Dennis went back to work. Communication wasn't much of a problem, with the help of computers and emails, but Dennis found that the side effects of many of his medicines left him terribly tired by midday. After several months, he began falling asleep in meetings, which obviously wasn't good for his job performance. One day he came to see me asking about Social Security Disability. I urged him to apply. He didn't want to be a "burden on society" in his own words, but I told him this was exactly what SSD was for: hard workers like himself who through no fault of their own were no longer able to work. He'd done his best—more than his best—but his handicaps were just too great. It took several months for me to convince him. He eventually did stop working and did receive Disability, though he and his wife had to declare bankruptcy a few months later. It was just one more indignity that he withstood with his characteristic good cheer.

Just as each visit with Dennis lifted my spirits, every time Mark showed up in the office they sank. Mark never stopped complaining, but he also never tried to do anything to take care of himself. Every now and then he would complain that his throat hurt and he was afraid his cancer had come back. But he was getting scans every six months that always showed him to be completely tumor-free. More than once I wondered why Dennis's cancer had recurred while Mark was still completely free of disease all these years later.

Somehow Dennis kept going. I saw him at least once a month to monitor the anticoagulant drugs that guarded the blood supply to the grafted flap that formed the floor of his mouth. He frequently came in between those visits complaining of a sense of swelling in his throat, for which I treated him. I enjoyed his visits very much. Despite never again being able to eat or speak normally, he seemed to enjoy his visits with me. Certainly he enjoyed watching his girls grow strong, smart, and lovely. But it was quite clear that he was in constant physical discomfort. Who the hell wouldn't be, with a tube in the stomach to eat through and another in the neck for breathing? He couldn't even lie flat to sleep; he spent his nights in a recliner in his family room.

One morning, less than one month before he turned 40, Dennis's wife found him dead in his recliner. Although an autopsy was performed, the cause of death was never determined for certain.

No evidence of recurrent cancer was found.

I went straight to the hospital when I got the call that he'd been brought in, partly to comfort his wife and partly to say a final good-bye for myself. After signing his death certificate and completing the paperwork, I drove slowly back to the office. I found myself fighting back tears, thinking about Dennis's suffering. I pulled myself together as I drove into the parking lot and entered through the back door. I stopped in my office and grabbed my stethoscope, then headed out to see who was first on the schedule that morning. It was Mark.

His throat was hurting him, but it looked fine on exam. His nose was stuffy and he had a cough; he stank of cigarette smoke. I was still so torn up about Dennis that I couldn't bring myself to get after Mark one more time about his ridiculously unhealthy lifestyle, nor to point out to him how lucky he was to have beaten the odds with his prolonged cancer survival. For some reason, he stopped coming to the office as frequently and eventually I lost track of him. I have no idea where he is today or what became of him.

B AD THINGS HAPPEN to good people.
Only the good die young.

What goes around comes around.

Nothing but platitudes that we spout as we try to make sense of a universe packed with injustice.

They don't help.

Why are young, healthy, good people like Dennis afflicted with diseases that produce dreadful deformity and suffering, while miserable, nasty curmudgeons seem to slip through life so much more easily? And why does the seeming unfairness of it all bother us so much?

What is justice or fairness when it comes to medicine anyway? Why is it so important to us that goodness be rewarded and evil—or whatever the opposite of our perception of "good" may be—be punished? The idea of karma, the Buddhist concept of moral causation, resonates through many cultures, including ours. If bad things happen to you—a cancer diagnosis, a surgical complication, or an adverse reaction to a drug—it must be because you are a bad person; either deep down inside, or in a previous life, or just somehow. Likewise, if you are lucky—if your cancer is small, localized, and easily treated and never comes back—it means that your good fortune must be deserved. The human mind does not tolerate randomness.

As physicians, we understand the truth intellectually: that there is no logic, no rhyme or reason, to illness, disease, and suffering. We've all seen good people get terrible diseases, do poorly, suffer, and die. We've all seen people whose choices in life we didn't respect—perhaps even found reprehensible—who enjoyed long, healthy lives. The entire discipline of pediatric oncology flies in the face of any concept of a just universe. As professionals, we tell ourselves that we stand aloof from the emotional onslaught; the sense of wrongness in the universe when a child, an innocent, or another individual perceived as "good" suffers. And yet, however much we may try to suppress them, the emotions are there. We can let them eat away at us, or we can acknowledge them as we try to deal with the reality that bad things really do happen to good people.

So how do we go about that emotional acknowledgment?

Do we physicians cry with patients? Sometimes. There have been numerous private and semi-public discussions about this topic among doctors both in person and on the Internet. On the one hand, it can be a powerful show of empathy, demonstrating our emotions to the patient and family. On the other hand, there is general agreement that the essence of professionalism is never losing control. Certainly no one condones out-and-out hysterical sobbing in front of our patients, but the consensus seems to be that occasionally becoming misty-eyed in the context of a difficult emotional situation is acceptable.

There is some danger in refusing to face our emotions. That is the dark path that leads to callousness and eventually burnout; hastened if we use alcohol or other substances to avoid the feelings. In a sense, there is danger even in experiencing our emotions. No one wants to be upset, yet as physicians it is our job to deal with sick and dying people.

Marcus Welby didn't have to do it every day, though. Neither do I. One of the advantages of family medicine is that because we deal with such a variety of problems, not everything is terrible every moment of every day. We have the opportunity to bond with our patients in good times, and this is what helps us through the bad ones.

Still, we are the physicians. We are the ones who can relieve suffering—sometimes; and defer death—for a while, perhaps. As a long-ago mentor once pointed out to me, we don't give patients their diseases. It is not our fault when bad things happen to good people, even when we are the ones bearing the bad news, performing the painful procedures, or prescribing the poisonous drugs. As basic as it may sound, that simple truth is much harder to keep in mind when we are sitting in a room with a man with no tongue.

But the biggest problem is that understanding the true randomness of disease can be a crushing burden. If someone like Dennis can develop cancer of the tongue for no logical reason that can be medically determined, why can't I? Why can't my child? If you spend your days and nights and months and years caring for the victims of motor vehicle crashes, how can you bring yourself to climb behind the wheel of a car at the end of the day?

One bit of primitive, magical thinking to which we all-too-human physicians fall prey is to believe that it can't happen to us because after all, we are physicians. We know how to prevent disease: don't smoke; wear your seatbelt and bike helmet; eat a balanced diet; exercise regularly; get plenty of sleep. We know what to do. Even if something were to happen, we know what to do about it. We can handle it. Thus do we keep at bay the fear of the unknown.

It is all too easy to confuse the power to diagnose and treat disease with the idea of power over the disease itself.

IT HAS BEEN SAID that the doctor who treats himself has a fool for a patient. I believe this; so, many years ago, I selected a doctor for myself and my family. He was a few years older than I. Calm, smart, funny, and caring, he was Marcus Welby incarnate. He was mentor and friend as well as physician and confidante. He was a wonderful person.

One Friday night I was at a worship service. One of the elements of the service was the recital of names of individuals in need of the community's support, usually because of illness or other infirmity. I was surprised to hear the name of my family doctor's son called out; he and his family were members of a different synagogue. The rabbi went on to briefly describe how the 13-year-old had been seriously injured in a motor vehicle accident. It sounded horrible, and I whispered a prayer for him.

After the service, I approached the rabbi and asked why the child's name had been included at our service. He told me that another family in our congregation were good friends and had asked to have them added to the list.

"I see," I said. "Two broken legs? That's so sad."

"Oh, yes," replied the rabbi. "It was a terrible accident. His father was killed."

My heart stopped. The rabbi had no way of knowing that I had any idea who "his father" was and what he meant to me. I felt as if my stomach had been ripped open and my guts yanked out, pooling on the sanctuary's carpeted floor.

It was hard to breathe. I just stood there as the rabbi moved on to another congregant.

How could my doctor be dead? I couldn't even remember exactly how old he was; was he even 40? How could this happen? He was a doctor. He couldn't die.

Somehow I found my way home. Somehow I made it through the days until the funeral, seeing patients without really seeing them; writing prescriptions mechanically; dispensing my usual advice as if on autopilot. I kept thinking about my doctor. He should be seeing his patients, writing prescriptions, and dispensing advice; not lying in a plain wooden casket awaiting his burial, even as his son struggled to recover from his injuries. With luck, the boy's legs would heal. But as keenly as I felt the loss of his father, I could barely imagine what this boy and his mother and sister were going through.

I cancelled my patient appointments the day of the funeral and dressed appropriately. It was a gorgeous autumn day, sunny with the last warmth of summer; too beautiful for this kind of occasion. The synagogue sat alone in an area that was just beginning to undergo development, surrounded by fields which were needed for all the cars that didn't fit in the parking lot. As I approached the building, I saw an ambulance pull up. The back doors were opened and a wheelchair containing a child was carefully extracted. Both of the boy's legs were supported straight out in front of him, clearly casted from surgery to repair the fractures.

I saw him wince as the attendants set the chair down on the sidewalk as gently as they could. As we filed into the sanctuary I saw almost all the doctors from the hospital at which I had done my training. Most of them looked as stunned as I felt.

I don't remember much about the service. It was mercifully short but still felt like an eternity. An eternity is exactly what it was: the beginning of life without my doctor. As upset as I was for myself, I realized that my loss was shared with the community that consisted of his other patients. We were all bereft, wondering what we would do without him.

I joined an extremely long line of cars that were headed to the cemetery. The synagogue was at the edge of town, but the burial was to be at the end of another 45-minute drive into the country. Again I was struck by the beautiful weather. A light breeze played over my face and I found myself wondering if this was the universe's way of trying to comfort me. Unscientific, perhaps, but I wasn't feeling particularly rational that day. The cemetery was on a steeper hillside than I would have thought advisable to use for this purpose. Small, terraced areas surrounded by trees revealed short rows of headstones. Because there were so many cars, many of us had to park well back from the grave. I got out of my car and walked along the black-topped road as it switch-backed its way around the hill, until the open grave and the mound of dirt with a shovel stuck into it came into view.

There was no microphone, and there were so many

people that I found myself standing too far back to hear the words. I didn't need to, though. As the familiar prayers and psalms were recited, I moved my lips along with the crowd, not trusting my voice. The coffin was lowered into the grave and, one by one, mourners filed forward to sprinkle a shovelful of dirt over its lid. The tradition is not to leave the graveside until the top of the coffin is completely covered. There were so many people who all wanted to help honor this kind, wonderful man that there was more than just one layer covering him by the time everyone had filed past the mound of dirt.

Finally the burial was completed and I returned to my car, alone with my thoughts. All that kept running through my head, over and over, was that bad things really do happen to good people; and there's not a damn thing that can be done about it.

# The better the surgeon, the more reluctant he is to operate.

*"If you only have a hammer,*
*you tend to see every problem as a nail."*
— Abraham Maslow

I ONCE HAD SOME PROBLEMS with the plumbing in my office, so I called a plumber. He came in and examined each fixture. Then he went down to the basement and carefully checked the pipes, following each one as they branched and spread to the bathrooms and exam room sinks, all the way back to where the main water trunk entered the building. Finally, after an exhaustive inspection of every aspect of my office's entire plumbing system, he took out a medium-sized wrench and went to a particular spot where a smaller pipe branched off another one. He fitted the tool around the joint and turned it 90 degrees.

"That should do it," he said.

I followed him back upstairs and sure enough, everything was working just fine. I thanked him effusively.

Then he handed me a bill for $200.

"What!?!" I said. "All you did was turn a fitting one-quarter of a turn! Do you expect me to pay you $200 just for that?"

"Of course not," he replied. "Here, give me that bill and I'll itemize it for you."

He scribbled something on the page and handed it back to me. Now it read:

"Adjust fitting: $5

"Knowing where and how much to turn: $195"

IN MEDICINE, THERE IS a sharp divide between knowing what to do and doing it. Nowadays, the dysfunctional payment system for American medicine remits significantly more for the doing than the knowing.

Diagnosis, the process of figuring out what is wrong, can often be complex and time-consuming. Talking to the patient, performing an examination, and ordering necessary tests are just the beginning. Interpreting the results isn't always straightforward. Deciding what to recommend and then explaining everything to the patient is a skill in and of itself. Not infrequently, the treatment plan includes a referral to another doctor who has skills different from mine. Who are these specialists, and how did they get to be the way they are?

WATCH A GROUP of medical students sitting around a table studying together, and you can tell who is going into which specialty.

"Can someone please pass me Robbin's?"

"But you've already got Nelson's and Harrison's open in front of you."

"I need to look up the pathophysiology of this patient's electrolyte imbalance."

"But your patient has a broken leg."

"But his sodium is 142 instead of 140 and I want to know why."

That's the student who has "specialist" written all over her. You just know she's going to go the extra mile, order the extra test, perform the extra procedure; all for the sake of certainty.

Next to her is a husky fellow wearing a college football jacket, tossing a wad of paper straight up in the air and catching it over and over as he recites the names of the bones in the wrist, "Scaphoid, lunate, triquetrum, pisiform, trapezium, trapezoid, capitates, hamate. C'mon, guys, give me a tougher one."

Clearly an orthopedist in the making.

The skinny guy with the wire-rimmed glasses is making flash cards of the cranial nerves: olfactory, optical, oculomotor, trochlear, trigeminal, abducens, facial, auditory, glossopharyngeal, vagus, accessory, hypoglossal.

Some people are just made for neurology.

Even without knowing what they're studying, you can identify their specialties by the way the students approach problems.

The "surgical" type is the guy (typically it's a male) who is impulsive, sure of himself, decisive, and willing to take chances. He is the action-oriented doctor whose motto is "Don't just stand there; do something." Anything. These people are quick to act because they are often in situations where quick action is the lifesaving thing to do. In appropriate settings such as trauma, emergency medicine, and (of course) the operating room, this mindset combined with their rigorous training serves them—and their patients—very well indeed. They tend to be impatient, coining aphorisms like "A chance to cut is a chance to cure," and "When in doubt, cut it out." If the problem isn't something they can fix, they're not interested.

Doctors who go into medicine (defined as "not surgery"), on the other hand, often work more slowly and deliberately. They are often more cautious and thorough, sometimes to the point of obsession. These are the physicians more willing to delve into a diagnostic dilemma; perhaps they're more tolerant of complexity. These clinicians are drawn to patients with many symptoms and multiple co-existing diseases; the patients who typically require the doctor to spend more time thinking, whose problems cannot be readily solved with a knife. And even as these practitioners slip through the years, a hint of nerdiness can continue to cling to them, like a tiny loose thread hanging off their long white coat.

THERE IS ANOTHER, more subtle but just as definite, divide between types of doctors.

"This patient has a fever, chills, and body aches that came on abruptly during the winter. What do you think is wrong?"

Doctor Specialist: "The differential diagnosis of fever includes infectious, metabolic, toxic, and neoplastic entities. We need to culture all his bodily fluids and do CT scans of his brain, chest, abdomen, and pelvis. Then we need to send blood for labs and toxicology screens. That will tell us what's wrong with him."

Doctor Generalist: "I think he has the flu."

Doctor S: "Well, sure, he could have the flu. But he could also have cancer, sepsis, or any of a thousand other things."

Doctor G: "True, but why don't we wait and see if he develops any other symptoms first, or if he just gets better on his own over the next seven to ten days."

Doctor S: "I suppose we could do that. But I'd like to know for sure."

This is the difference between the generalist and the specialist. It's been described many ways: the difference between lateral and vertical thinking; broad versus narrow thinking; the overview versus the detail; the landscape versus the miniature. Probably the biggest difference between the two is their tolerance for uncertainty. The specialist must leave no stone unturned, no reference unchecked, no test unordered, just to be sure. More than just the compulsive need to get every exam question correct, it is the urge for "completeness" that sometimes goes beyond what the patient needs to be correctly diagnosed and effectively treated.

Marcus Welby and I are generalists. Although we are indeed precise and thorough, at the end of the day we are willing to go to bed without requiring the complete certainty of a definitive diagnosis. After making sure the patient is at no immediate risk, we are able to wield the most powerful tool in our diagnostic armamentarium: time. Every disease has its natural course. Many illnesses will resolve on their own without any medical intervention. Others require treatment of some kind, although often the difference between the two isn't immediately obvious. Our greater patience helps us recognize that much about a patient's condition will eventually become clear. Why put a patient through an extensive and costly battery of tests and diagnostic procedures when time will tell?

A SIDE FROM HAVING the compulsive attitude that specializing requires, which is probably present at birth, how do specialists get that way?

It starts with four years of medical school—years that seem interminable while you slog through them, soaking up an overwhelming amount of material. By the time you graduate, you feel as if your brain has absorbed every last piece of information that can possibly fit into it. You take your last exam and feel as if you've just spewed all that information back out onto the answer sheet, leaving nothing inside your head. Then you go out, have a beer and a good night's sleep, and are ready to begin the next stage of your education, in which you actually learn to do whatever it is you've chosen to do for the rest of your medical career.

Postgraduate education is known as residency training, a holdover from the days when trainees actually resided in the hospital. Back in the 1950s, when Marcus Welby was in training, every medical student's first year was the same. It was called a rotating internship, because each new physician spent the year rotating through each of the major medical fields of medicine, surgery, pediatrics, and obstetrics/gynecology. After that, many young physicians went out into the world and hung out their shingle, practicing on their own or in small groups. They called themselves General Practitioners. Their compatriots who chose to pursue more advanced training in one medical field or another stayed on in the hospital for another stint that lasted anywhere from three to five more years. Personal lives were frowned upon during residency training; the study of medicine was supposed to be all-consuming. The final reward for this monastic existence was the role of specialist, their extra income and prestige felt by all to be well-earned.

As medical knowledge advanced, training adapted. By the 1960s it was recognized that being a generalist was in many ways just as challenging as practicing specialty medicine. Learning how to sort out the symptoms of any given patient who may walk in off the street, not only differentiating between what was going to get better on its own and what needed medical intervention but also determining which of the exploding number of new interventions were appropriate, had truly become a full-time specialty of its own. It was re-named family practice. It developed its own residency training programs that now lasted three years. Paradoxically, everyone was now a "specialist." The American Board of Family Medicine (originally called the American Board of Family Practice) was recognized in 1969 and gave its first qualifying examination in 1970, giving rise to the era of the Board-certified generalist.

Medical advances necessitated changes in specialist training as well. So many new procedures were developed that it was no longer possible to become a true expert in one entire organ system. Specialties shattered into sub-specialties, each with a scope of practice as narrow as shards of broken glass, each requiring years of extra training.

Cardiology, ophthalmology, neurology, and orthopedics have each become thoroughly subdivided into their own tiny niches, where the best of specialists still are the ones most reluctant to operate.

No LONGER IS it good enough for me just to send a heart patient to a cardiologist. Now I need to determine precisely what part of the heart is malfunctioning in order to choose just the right specialist.

"Mr. Bishop, I heard a murmur when I listened to your heart today, so I'd like to send you for an echocardiogram."

"What's that, Doctor?"

"It's a picture of your heart made with sound waves. It will tell us what's causing the murmur."

"What kinds of things could be causing it?"

"Your heart has little flaps of tissue called valves that prevent the blood from flowing backward. If one of those valves is too tight, or if it leaks, the turbulence of the abnormal blood flow causes the murmur. Depending on how bad it is, you might need surgery to fix or replace the valve."

"Well, I certainly don't want that!"

"No one does, Mr. Bishop, but the echocardiogram is the only way to know for sure."

"Does it hurt?"

"Not at all. The technician just runs a microphone over your chest. Nothing to it."

I HAVE ANOTHER PATIENT who has palpitations.

"Doctor, I have these terrible episodes where my heart seems to be pounding out of my chest. It races so fast, I get scared."

"Well, Mr. Einthoven, your heart monitor shows that your heart rhythm is irregular at times and that's what's causing your discomfort."

"What do you mean my rhythm is irregular? Is my heart going to stop beating?"

"No, not at all. In order for your heart to beat properly, all of the individual muscle cells must contract together in a coordinated fashion. Otherwise each fiber of muscle would beat at its own rate and your heart would look like a ball of jiggling worms. The electrical signal that triggers a coordinated contraction starts in a group of specialized nerve cells at the top of the heart's right atrium. These nerve cells send the impulse through tissues specially adapted to conduct electricity; the heart's wiring, so to speak. Sometimes there's a short-circuit or an extra pathway that's disrupting the signal."

"What can you do about it, Doctor?"

"I'm going to send you to a cardiologist who specializes in electrophysiology."

"What can he do about it?"

"He can do lots of things. He may decide to give you a pacemaker."

"What's that?"

"It's a tiny, battery-powered device implanted under the skin of your chest with wires leading into your heart. Older pacemakers just sent regular impulses to regulate the heartbeat, but the newer ones read the heart's own electrical activity and fire only when necessary. The most advanced models can even deliver an electric shock to start your heart back up again if the rhythm becomes dangerously unstable."

"What if it's not that bad? Are there other things he can do to help?"

"He can thread a tiny tube called a catheter through an artery in your groin up into your heart. Then, through the tube, he feeds wires into your heart muscle that can locate the abnormal tissue and destroy it with electricity."

"Wow. That sounds hard."

"Well, the electrophysiologists are very good."

AND THEN THERE'S the patient with angina, whose chest pain shows that he is at risk for a heart attack.

"I'm going to send you to the interventional cardiologist, Mr. Black."

"What can she do for me, Doctor?"

"She can take you to the catheterization laboratory and thread a tube up into your heart. Then she can inject dye and take pictures of your blood vessels to see which ones are blocked and how badly. She may even be able to open them up by threading a balloon over a wire through the blockage and inflating the balloon to crush the obstruction. She may have to insert a mesh-like stent to support the vessel so it doesn't close back up, but then you won't have a heart attack because the blockage will be gone."

"What if she can't?"

"Well, she might recommend bypass surgery, or she may suggest that we just treat you with medicines."

"Whatever you think best, Doc."

THE BETTER THE SPECIALISTS, the fewer procedures they do. I've learned the hard way to nail down the patient's cardiac diagnosis as specifically as I can before sending him to just the right cardiology subspecialist. Too many general cardiologists these days take a "shotgun" approach to diagnosis, sending every patient for an echocardiogram, a 24-hour rhythm monitor, and a nuclear stress test, regardless of the presenting complaint. As long as doctors are paid more for doing than for thinking, procedures are what you're going to get.

SEVERAL YEARS AGO I was at an ophthalmology conference when I got something in my eye. *How fortunate*, I thought. *Here I am, surrounded by hundreds of eye doctors. Surely it will be easy enough to find someone to help me.*

I stopped the first conference participant I encountered.

"Excuse me, Doctor, but I think I have something in my eye. Can you help me get it out?"

"No, sorry. I'm a glaucoma specialist. I spend my time

taking care of patients with high pressure behind their corneas. Either the eye makes too much fluid, or there's some kind of blockage in the drainage system in the angle of the cornea. My specialized training lets me perform laser surgery to unblock the system, though I'm also an expert in prescribing eyedrops to lower the pressure."

"Why can't you help me?"

"Because I don't remember anything about how to get something out of the eye. Sorry."

I moved on to the next person.

"Excuse me, Doctor, but I have something in my eye. Can you help me?"

"No, sorry. I'm a cornea specialist. I spend all day doing delicate surgery that changes the curvature of the cornea so that patients can have improved vision without glasses or contact lenses. I also perform corneal transplants for people with severe damage. Restoring sight to the blind is incredibly rewarding. Unfortunately, I'm not comfortable trying to get something out of your eye without my special equipment. Sorry."

I held my hand over my eye as I searched out someone else.

"Doctor, can you help me get something out of my eye?"

"No. I'm a retina specialist. I deal only with the tissues at the back of the eye. If the blood vessels in your retina were proliferating and threatening your vision because of diabetes, you'd be in luck. I could do laser surgery to limit the damage and stop you from going blind. And if the macula—the dense collection of visual receptors in the center of the retina that are responsible for fine pinpoint vision—was degenerating, I'd be just the person to help you. But I haven't dealt with anything at the front of the eye for decades. Sorry I can't help."

I tried to find someone else. My eye was beginning to really hurt.

"Excuse me, Doctor. Could you please help me get something out of my eye?"

"Sorry. I only do eye muscle surgery. Sometimes patients with crossed eyes need an operation to adjust the muscles so that their eyes will work together again. That's my specialty."

Now I was getting desperate.

"Excuse me, Doctor. Can you help me with my eye?"

"No. I'm a neuro-ophthalmologist. Is there anything wrong with the optic nerve at the back of your eye? It carries information from your retina to your brain."

"Yes, I know. No, there's nothing wrong with my optic nerves that I know of. I just have something in my eye."

"Why don't you go to the restroom and run some water in it? I learned that in a Boy Scout First Aid class when I was 12."

"Oh! I suppose I could do that."

So I did, and my eye felt fine. It was a good thing I was

at a convention of eye doctors. There's nothing like consulting a specialist.

I'VE NEVER MET a neurologist who didn't order an electroencephalogram (an EEG, a recording of the electrical activity of the brain) and an MRI on every patient.

"Doctor Parkinson, I'm sending you a patient with migraine headaches. I'm perfectly comfortable treating her, but she insists on seeing a neurologist."

"I'd be happy to see her. Have you gotten an MRI of her brain and an EEG?"

"Um, no. Her neurological exam is completely normal. There are no other symptoms suggestive of a brain tumor or something anatomically wrong with her central nervous system. She's never had anything that sounds like seizure activity. Why does she need an MRI and EEG?"

"Because I'm a neurologist. I treat the brain and the central nervous system. The MRI tells me what it looks like and the EEG tells me how it's functioning."

Hammers and nails; MRIs and EEGs.

I'VE ALSO NEVER MET an orthopedist who didn't order an x-ray.

Most patients have two arms and two legs, each with three long bones and two large joints apiece. There are 27 bones in each hand; 26 in each foot. Add in the 24 vertebrae that make up the spine and you have a target-rich environment for an x-ray machine. These bones connect to each other in a variety of ways, from the simple hinge of the knee and elbow to the ball and socket of the hip and shoulder. The bones of the spine are interspersed with fibrous tissue that provide cushioning but little movement. Wherever bone meets bone there is a protective layer of cartilage and a capsule of gristle-like fibrous tissue holding the joint together. Ligaments support the connections between bones; tendons attach muscle to bone; all of which is how muscular contractions are translated into bending and straightening, flexion and extension, back and forth, over and over, as we move through the world.

Any time something hurts, be it a neck or back, arm or leg, knee or ankle, finger or toe, the orthopod will "take a picture." It's what they do, even when they don't have to.

"Doctor, I hurt my ankle. Do I need an x-ray?"

"Can you walk on the ankle?"

"Yes, but it hurts."

"That's okay. Could you walk on it right after you hurt it?"

"Yes, but I limped a little."

"That's fine. Does it hurt here or here?" I ask, pushing on the bony bumps called the lateral and medial malleoli on the outside and inside of the ankle.

"No."

"How about here?" I ask, pressing again on each side, this time about three inches higher.

"No."

"Then you don't need an x-ray."

"How do you know?"

"Because a group of doctors in Ottawa did some very extensive studies of people with ankle injuries. They figured out that if you can bear some weight on an injured ankle, and if the tips of the malleoli and the area about three inches up the ankle don't hurt when someone presses on them, then the chances of you having a significant fracture of your ankle are small enough that you don't need an x-ray."

"Okay. But do I need to see an orthopedist?"

"Not really. I can take care of your sprained ankle for you, but if you really want to see the orthopedist, you can."

"Good. Maybe he'll take an x-ray."


PULMONOLOGISTS—LUNG DOCTORS—perform lung function tests. It's what they do.

"Doctor, I'm so sorry I didn't come to you for this problem, but my employer insisted that I see their specialist for my positive tuberculosis test."

"That's okay, Mrs. Ayer; I don't mind. Tuberculosis usually affects the lungs."

"Well, *I* mind. Before I even saw the doctor, the first thing they did was take me into a little room and make me blow into all these machines. Why did they do that?"

"I don't know. Do you want me to call his office and find out?"

"Yes, please. I'd really like to know."

Trudge out to the phone; call the pulmonology office; follow the robot's instruction to "press 1" because I am a doctor or a hospital—and I still end up speaking to a secretary.

"Excuse me, I'm the primary physician for Mrs. Ayer. She was in your office last week for a positive PPD at her place of employment. She has no lung complaints. Can you please tell me why you did pulmonary function tests on her?"

"Oh, the doctor has us do them on every patient before he even sees them. He is a pulmonologist, you know."

Oh, how well I know.


I'VE ALSO NEVER MET a rheumatologist who doesn't order a ton of blood work.

Common things are common. This common-sense common knowledge is contained in the old aphorism, "When you hear hoofbeats, think horses and not zebras."

There are indeed times when a diagnosis is unusual or rare. Thanks to that old saying, those conditions are called "zebras."

"Mrs. Berger, you have a condition called polymyalgia rheumatica. That's why you're so tired and why you have pain in your upper arms and legs."

"Are you sure, Doctor?"

"Yes, I am. The only abnormality on your blood tests was a sky-high sedimentation rate that dropped immediately with a low dose of prednisone."

"That medicine was amazing! I was feeling so much better overnight!"

"Yes, I know. That's another reason I'm confident that we have the right diagnosis. Still, I'd like to send you to a rheumatologist. It's not a difficult diagnosis to make, but they have more experience treating it than I do."

"Certainly, Doctor. And thank you!"

Days pass.

The patient sees the specialist.

More days pass, and the patient returns to my office.

"What can I do for you today, Mrs. Berger?"

"I just need some blood work for the rheumatologist."

I peruse the slip she hands me, which orders 14 exotic blood tests to rule out every other rheumatologic disease I've ever heard of, and some that I think he must have made up.

"Why are you shaking your head, Doctor?"

"I'm just thinking. I suppose a specialist can be defined as the doctor who, when presented with a horse, still goes looking for the zebra."

WHEN I WAS IN medical school, I once overheard a surgeon asking a resident what he would do for a particular patient. I got the impression that the resident wasn't entirely familiar with the patient in question but was trying to wing it.

"I'd perform an appendectomy," he answered.

"An appendectomy?" shrieked the attending surgeon.

"This is a 17-year-old girl with a broken arm! Why on earth do you want to do an appendectomy?"

Undeterred, the resident answered with a surprising degree of poise: "I am a surgeon. Surgeons do what they do best. Appendectomy is what I do best."

THROUGHOUT THEIR LONG and arduous training, all specialists strive to be the best. It's what they do.

But they can only be the best at what they do. Everything else is someone else's problem. Figuring out which specialist is best—if one is needed at all—for any given patient who walks in off the street is no job for a specialist. That's *my* job. It is my calling, because I have more than just a hammer. I have a complete tool kit consisting of my eyes, my ears, and my hands; my training, my experience, and my expertise that I bring to bear on every medical problem I face. Make no mistake: I value the expertise offered by my specialist colleagues. We need each other to care for our patients. But the specialists who are most useful to me—and to my patients—are the ones with the keenest understanding of their limitations; the ones willing to say, "I don't know"; the surgeons most reluctant to operate.

# Part A: It has to be fun.
# Part B: If it isn't fun,
# see Part A.

I MADE THE DECISION early in my life that fun was very important to me. Given that I had also decided on medicine as a career, it meant that the education and training process was going to be long and drawn-out. Finding a way to have fun through all those years was a challenge. To meet it, I had to be creative. Fortunately, I also got lucky. Then again, it has been frequently observed that creativity and luck often tend to go together.

It began in college. I had decided when I was in third grade that I wanted to be a doctor, so upon enrolling in college I could immediately have declared my major to be "pre-med." There were two problems with this. The first was that I truly loved biology, and wanted to pursue it as my major area of study. The second was that the college I had chosen didn't have "pre-med" as a formally recognized major. So I began my studies in biology, along with the required pre-medical science curriculum. And it was a helluva lot of fun—the subject matter was absorbing and intriguing, and I was eager and happy to immerse myself in it.

The second semester of the introductory biology course was devoted to genetics. The accompanying laboratory course, designed to give us a hands-on understanding of the concepts presented in the lectures, revolved around the genetics of the venerable fruit fly, or as we came to know it, *Drosophila melanogaster.* These little buggers are about an eighth of an inch long, have big red eyes, and ask nothing more from life than food, which the lab supplied in the form of a sticky, slanted glob at the bottom of a glass tube. Stoppered with a bit of sponge to let air in but keep the flies from getting out, these little glass vials served as perfectly adequate homes for up to a dozen or two *D. melanogaster* specimens at a time. If you soaked the stopper with ether, you could render all the flies in the vial unconscious for a while. This let you pour them out onto a piece of paper and, using pointy little instruments, maneuver them under a dissecting microscope (sort of a high-power, freestanding magnifying glass) and sort through them.

Most of our fruit flies had red eyes, but some carried a

mutant gene that made their eyes brown. Others had mutations that left them with curly wings instead of regular ones,
but you had to be careful to place the vials that contained
those curly-wing flies on their sides; if the vials were upright
the curly-wings would get stuck in their food and die. Under
the dissecting microscope you could identify the flies' gen-
ders. Males had black, hook-like graspers on their front
limbs; females didn't.

If you took an empty vial and added a mixture of male
and female fruit flies, they would make like the birds and
the bees, which in their case would result in more fruit
flies. The part of the fruit-fly life cycle most salient to our
purposes in genetics lab was that female fruit flies were
fertile within about 12 hours of hatching from their pupal
stage. To be safe, we were taught that they didn't mate until
they were at least eight hours old. Thus, if you emptied a
glass vial that was previously occupied by a mixture of fertile
flies, any females that hatched in the next eight hours were
guaranteed not to have already mated. This was important
for genetics experiments in which we intentionally matched
males with one mutation to females with a different mutation, then calculated the incidences of the combinations
of the mutations in their progeny. In order to obtain virgin
female fruit flies with which to perform these experiments,
the lab was open to us 24 hours a day, and we were expected
to plan our activities accordingly.

I was a college student. I was determined to have fun

other than that related to my classes. I took my studies seriously, but I took my collegiate pleasures seriously too. I made a point of taking at least one night off every week from studying—usually Friday, as that was movie night. Sometimes I would visit friends at other nearby colleges who took their fun just as seriously. I tried not to let the fruit-fly lab cramp my style, though I thoroughly enjoyed trying to explain the lab to other students, especially those who weren't majoring in the sciences.

"Yikes!" I would say, looking at my watch and noting that six hours had elapsed since I had last emptied an experimental fruit-fly vial. "I have to go! I have to get back to the lab before the fruit flies lose their virginity." (That's not what I really said. Instead of "lose their virginity" I actually used a single-syllable word of Anglo-Saxon derivation that means "copulate" and alliterates with "fruit flies.") Off we'd fly, driving along deserted roads in the dead of night, hollering out the windows, "Got to get to the fruit flies before they lose their virginity." (Or something more alliterative.)

That was fun.

Lectures weren't always as much fun, though the professor did his best. He was an aging hippie (probably younger then than I am now) who wore jeans and t-shirts to lectures. One day, as he was expounding on something chromosomal, I heard a murmur pass through the room. The student next to me nudged me and said, "Look at his shirt."

The professor was wearing a white t-shirt with what appeared to be an abstract design on it. He was moving around as he spoke, so it was difficult to get a clear look at it, but as he turned to make a point I suddenly realized that it was a pen-and-ink line drawing of a pair of fruit flies copulating! I smothered my giggle, and turned to see who else was aware of this fact. By then, it seemed everyone was. Eventually, the professor became aware of our collective state of suppressed hilarity and turned to address us.

"You're all snickering because you think sex is dirty." He paused for a moment as if he had finished, but in fact he was just letting the giggles build. Then, as he turned back to the chalkboard, he added, "It is, by the way, if you do it properly."

That was fun, too.

Although my college had no formal pre-med major, it did provide all the necessary preparation for medical school. In addition to the required science and lab courses, we received registration information for the medical school aptitude test that was required for med school admission: the MCAT. Back then, as today, the MCAT was a very big deal. There were so many applicants for each medical school opening that it was vital to achieve excellent MCAT scores. Then, as now, I didn't worry. I've always been a good test-taker; filling in those little ovals with #2 pencils was always fun for me. (Even my most recent experience with standardized testing, almost 30 years later, now on a computer instead of with #2 pencils, was a pleasure. I passed this latest test with a score of over 90% too.)

In all honesty, after all these years I don't remember much about the MCAT itself. Still, the day is stuck firmly in my memory for the following reason: I had the most amazing sandwich during the MCAT lunch break.

I found a small delicatessen and ordered a roast beef sandwich. I asked for white bread and butter, and decided to try Havarti cheese, which I had never tasted.

What a sandwich!

Each slice of bread was at least an inch thick. The butter, slathered thickly, was unsalted, just the way I like it. The roast beef was bloody rare; perfect. The mellow, creamy flavor of the Havarti was amazing; I'd found a new favorite. The whole sandwich was so thick I could barely get it into my mouth. As hard as I've tried since, I've never been able to replicate that sandwich. All these years later, I still salivate just thinking about it.

That was fun.

MOVING ON TO medical school was also fun. Sure, there was a lot of work, but it wasn't difficult conceptually. There was just a lot of material. Through it all, I was fortunate to find friends who felt as I did: that there was always time for recreation. Each spring we unshackled ourselves from studying long enough to enjoy the official first picnic of the season. In winter we ran across snow-covered fields at night (inducing the occasional attack of exercise-induced asthma, exacerbated by the cold air, even though we weren't yet aware of it as a clinical entity).

The first two years of medical school consisted mostly of sitting in lecture halls, listening to, of all things, lectures. There were no assigned seats, yet within a few weeks we had all de facto selected our places from which we rarely strayed. It was a small enough class that by the end of the first semester I knew all my classmates by name. Even those who didn't sit near me I considered friends. When we weren't warming our self-assigned lecture-hall seats, we had various labs. Gross anatomy in the first year wasn't a lot of fun, though it was fascinating. Later labs were much more enjoyable. By the end of the first year I felt as comfortable looking through a microscope as I was looking through my own glasses.

The third year saw us split up into small groups as we went out onto the hospital floors, rotating through the various medical disciplines, each of which was great fun, albeit in very different ways.

Every medical student loves surgery. It's as if the adrenaline of the operating room is addictive. We learned the ritual of scrubbing one's hands for ten minutes by watching the residents and attending surgeons as they carefully lathered up, then methodically scrubbed each side of each finger a predefined number of times. It was important to hold the elbows below the hands while rinsing, so that dirty water from the unscrubbed parts of the arms didn't drip back over the more carefully cleansed hands and fingers. The hardest part was learning not to mind water dripping from our elbows onto the floor. The art of reaching out for a sterile towel with which to dry the hands and arms was trickier than it looked. We had to hold the towel far enough away so that it never touched our unsterile clothing, even though that clothing consisted of clean scrub suits we had just changed into that morning. This was followed by the dance of donning a sterile gown and plunging our hands into latex gloves held out by a nurse—all without "contaminating" ourselves by touching an unsterile surface. Once I got the hang of it, it was great fun.

Surgery itself was fascinating—watching as the intact body surface lying before me was transformed by a carefully made surgical wound; seeing the incision extended and deepened as, one by one, the layers into whatever body cavity was being opened were cut and divided, until finally the internal anatomy was exposed. One of the most interesting operations I observed was for a perforated peptic ulcer. As the surgeons made their way into the abdomen and exposed the stomach, I saw a small hole—no bigger than a quarter of an inch. This tiny defect had brought the patient to the hospital in such severe pain that his entire abdominal wall was literally as hard as a board, his muscles trying to guard his damaged gut. I watched with admiration and amazement as the surgeons covered the hole over, completing their procedure and curing the patient.

Obstetrics was just as much fun, in an awe-inspiring way.

There is nothing more miraculous than being present at the birth of a baby. All the clichés about "the wonder of a new life" are true. First the top of the head comes into view—often covered with hair visible through the layer of waxy white vernix that protects the fetal skin in utero—followed by its gradual emergence until, with the mother's final push, the head emerges completely. It is a magical moment. Here the doctor must intrude, suctioning out the baby's mouth and nose to clear the airway before he takes his first breath. I later learned that the next step was checking to make sure the umbilical cord wasn't wrapped around the baby's neck, followed by a gentle tug downward to deliver the baby's first shoulder, then upward so the other shoulder can emerge. At this point the arms pop out, and the infant usually looks surprised. With outspread arms, he looks like he is embracing the world even before he has fully entered it. The rest of the body slides out, and the first thing everyone looks at is the crotch, so as to make the all-important announcement about the baby's gender. Of course, the doctor is also watching closely to make sure the baby is breathing; the frequent healthy wail is reassuring on that score. Those attending the birth are also watching to make certain the baby's bluish color turns to pink fairly rapidly, as oxygen floods the lungs for the first time and the newborn circulation quickly adjusts to the new source of the vital gas.

Before I had full responsibility for deliveries, what I found most touching was the expressions on the faces of the parents as they saw and held their new baby for the first time. The joy, tenderness, amazement, awe, all at the same time; the sheer depth of emotion at that instant is transcendent. It is humbling to watch, to share the moment a family is formed and a new human joins the world. Later on, as I sat in the nursery completing the ubiquitous paperwork, the grandparents, aunts, uncles, and other extended family would appear in the corridor outside the nursery. The babies were lined up in front of the window in their bassinets, a pink or blue name tag visible above each infant's head. The visitors wandered up and down the row until they found the one they sought: their newest relative, flesh of their flesh and blood of their blood. The same indescribable, universal emotions beamed from them. They were often moved to tears. I always was and I still am, just thinking about it.

That was great fun.

Logically following obstetrics, of course, comes pediatrics. Children are lots of fun, once you get used to them. Getting used to children was the goal of the third-year rotation in pediatrics.

One block of the pediatrics rotation was spent in the newborn nursery. Handling a brand-new baby takes some practice, and I remember precisely when I attained proficiency in that particular skill. It was a Saturday morning on call, which meant that the only people taking care of the babies in the nursery that day were me and one other upper-level pediatrics resident. There were about 12 babies, each of whom needed to be examined daily while in the hospital, so the resident and I got down to business.

For the first time, I was handling the babies all by myself, with no one looking over my shoulder. These were healthy newborns who had already been examined several times by fully qualified pediatricians and been declared to be completely normal, so the chances of me discovering any abnormalities were small. I was pretty sure the resident would be repeating the exam as well, so this was basically practice for me.

To perform the physical examination as I had been taught, I had to lift the infants, turn them over, undress them, examine them, and then replace their tiny shirts and diapers when my examination was complete. I didn't yet have children myself, so I struggled as I learned how to pull a firmly bent arm gently out of a long sleeve. I listened to the babies' tiny chests with one of the miniature neonatal stethoscopes that hung on the back of the nursery doors for common use. I looked in their little ears, and I struggled to get them to open their eyes so I could look into them too. I learned how to hold the legs together in one hand while using the other to palpate the abdomen, always mindful of the moist, jelly-like stump of the umbilical cord under the plastic clamp that always seemed to get in the way of what I was trying to feel. I examined the infants' hips to make sure the ball-and-socket joints had developed properly, learning about the clicks and clunks that may indicate when they hadn't. The babies didn't like that part much, and they not infrequently indicated their displeasure by gifting me with the contents of their bowels, their bladders, or both. So I also learned to take a stack of 4×4-inch gauze pads moistened in warm water and use them one by one to gently cleanse the diaper area, making sure to wipe all the nooks and crannies; and then I learned how to diaper a baby.

The first few times I lifted the infants, their heads flopped alarmingly. I quickly got the hang of supporting each little head with my fingers as I lifted the body, but what I found most interesting about the process was how efficiently I learned, without anyone else hanging over me, warning me constantly to support the head. From that experience, I came to realize that learning to handle a baby requires two things: a baby, and complete privacy. Years later, in my practice, this is what I tell new parents; fathers in particular. I reassure the mothers that the baby won't break—after all, I didn't break any in the nursery that day. The father doesn't need the mother gasping, "Watch the head!" every time he picks the kid up. The head's first flop drives the lesson home just as well.

That was fun.

Another incident during my pediatrics rotation was more fun to recall afterwards than it was while it was happening.

The definitive pediatrics textbook is *Nelson's Textbook of Pediatrics*, or simply "Nelson's." Originally edited by Waldo Nelson, MD, this doorstop of a tome was and is considered required reading by anyone needing to know anything and everything about pediatrics. It happened that one day, I and my fellow students on the pediatrics rotation had the unique honor of hosting a very distinguished visitor indeed: none other than Dr. Waldo Nelson himself.

Dr. Nelson would be rounding with the residents in the morning, but later in the afternoon he would be meeting with about 16 of us to discuss anything we wanted to know about pediatrics. Amazing! The actual editor of the ultimate pediatric textbook meeting with a small group of medical students to answer our questions; to lead a clinical discussion; to enlighten us on everything there was to know about the diagnosis and medical treatment of children. A living legend! It was enough to take our breath away.

While Dr. Nelson was occupied with the residents on the day of his visit, our attending physician took us aside and made certain we understood just how momentous this occasion was. She needn't have worried. We were a respectful group, well aware of the privilege about to be bestowed upon us.

After lunch, the attending brought Dr. Nelson to the fifth-floor conference room where we had already assembled, and introduced him to us.

This was in the early 1980s and at that time, suffice it

to say, Dr. Nelson was no spring chicken. The attending excused herself and left us with this very distinguished, very dapper, very elderly gentleman standing at the head of the conference table. He was of medium height, but stooped over, as the elderly often are. His exquisitely tailored three-piece suit hung a bit slack on his gaunt figure. His mind was completely intact; his answers to our questions were sharp and to the point. Unfortunately, I do not remember a word he said. In fact, I clearly remember not being able to concentrate on one word he was saying. You see, this distinguished, elderly, living legend whose name was synonymous with the bible of pediatrics was standing before us in his dapper three-piece suit... with his fly unzipped.

The struggle to keep a straight face, to remain respectful, to at least appear to be paying attention to what he was saying, all the while desperately trying to ignore his wardrobe malfunction, was agony. Should one of us have gone up to him, turned him around, and quietly informed him of what was awry? Probably; but at the time, it just seemed too difficult.

Later on, though, telling the story was fun.

GRADUATING FROM medical school, of course, was fun. Graduations always are. Residency training wasn't quite as much fun.

Residents' hours were long. Staying at the hospital all night every third or fourth night wasn't fun. But in a way, it was the same as the third year of medical school all over again. The first year of family practice residency consists of rotating through each of the five major areas in the hospital: surgery, emergency medicine, obstetrics/gynecology, pediatrics, and medicine. We also did a two-month rotation on the family practice service where we basically functioned as hospitalists, taking care of family practice office patients who needed hospital admission.

But there was also the office. What differentiates family medicine training from that of other specialties is its emphasis on outpatient training; specifically, on teaching physicians about taking care of patients in the office, as opposed to seeing only those who are sick enough to need hospitalization. As our training progressed, we spent more and more hours each week in the office taking care of our own patients.

With five residents per year and five major hospital areas, each resident was on a different service every two months. During our nights on call, though, we were expected to cover the entire hospital. Obviously, due to the sequencing of rotations, this meant that in the early parts of the year we had to cover areas through which we hadn't yet rotated. This led to some extra stress, especially for those of us who ended up doing some of the more specialized rotations earlier in the year.

Those of us who began with rotations in medicine, family practice, or emergency medicine quickly began learning the basic management of the most common problems that brought people to the hospital. Chest pain that might be heart attacks, gastrointestinal bleeding, pneumonia and the like were the sorts of things we began learning how to manage in the hospital setting.

On the other hand, if you began with obstetrics your days were filled with laboring women. You learned how to do vaginal exams to evaluate how dilated the cervix is—to give you a general idea of when the baby is going to be arriving—as well as all the mechanics of performing the delivery itself. These are not easy tasks. They take practice, and can be bewildering at the beginning of training. Thus, the overheard complaint of one of my friends who had started with obstetrics:

"You're all talking about orders to rule out heart attack, and I'm just worrying about why I can't find this guy's cervix."

That wasn't fun for him, but it was funny.

After the first year, the rotations during the next two years lasted one month apiece. Each rotation consisted of following a different specialist around wherever patients were seen, be it office, hospital, operating room, or any combination thereof. I found the offices to be the most fun, almost certainly because I identified myself as an office physician. I learned a lot on those rotations, although often what I learned was that I wanted to do things differently. It goes to prove that seeing a bad example can be just as educational as seeing a good one.

I admit that I struggled when things weren't as much fun. Rotations seemed to go on forever, with endless and unreasonable demands from patients and attending physicians, and a beeper that took on a life of its own, refusing to grant a moment's peace. That's when Part B of the Seventh Law applies: "When it isn't fun, see Part A" (It has to be fun). This is my formulation of the universal truth that nothing lasts—bad times or good times. When things are tough, it's difficult but important to remember that they won't always be so. I also think it's important to realize that the good times don't last either. Nothing does. So I try to make the most of all the good times as well, both in being mindful of and thankful for them, and to have as much fun as I can while I can. This served me well for much of the time through those two years, though I remained acutely aware that after residency training, I'd be on my own. It would be entirely up to me to make it fun.

Certainly the second two years had their funny moments.

Each week, the two residents on the family practice hospital service rotation presided over a conference where they gave presentations on all their patients to the rest of the trainees. We then proceeded to have a free-wheeling discussion about those patients and what the residents in charge of them ought to do for them. Despite the fact that these meetings occurred on Friday afternoons, they were prime examples of Monday morning quarterbacking.

One such conference included a presentation on an elderly man who had marginal social support (he was either homeless or nearly so) and had been admitted to the hospital with congestive heart failure. Part of the required admission ritual had included the history and complete physical examination, including a rectal exam. (It was drilled into us in medical school that there were only two acceptable reasons for omitting the rectal exam: no rectum or no finger.) Unfortunately, the admitting resident had noted that the patient had an abnormal prostate gland, and, one thing having led to another, the patient had been diagnosed with prostate cancer. Treatment options had been discussed with the urologists, and a recommendation had been made for hormone therapy. The patient, however, was now exhibiting signs of depression.

The prostate is a walnut-shaped gland at the base of the male bladder, easily accessible to the examining finger on rectal exam. The prostate secretes fluid in which sperm are suspended prior to and during ejaculation, and it becomes cancerous in pretty much every man who lives long enough. Given the masculinity of its function, it should come as no surprise that its growth and function are supported by male hormones. Because cancer is a state of uncontrolled growth, it makes sense that cancer of the prostate is potentiated by male hormones. Thus, hormone therapy for prostate cancer can take one of two forms: decrease the male hormones; and/or administer female hormones, which, unsurprisingly, oppose the action of male hormones.

In this patient's case, the recommendation for hormone therapy was to remove the source of male hormones by means of an orchiectomy: surgical removal of the testicles.

After the patient's presentation on this particular Friday, discussion flowed around the table. The man's congestive heart failure had been successfully treated; all that was left was the depression and the prostate cancer. Conversation centered on how best to treat the patient's depression. Drugs were suggested, as was psychotherapy. Finally the senior resident on the family practice service spoke up.

"Look, this guy comes into the hospital for his heart, and now we want to cut his nuts off. No wonder he's depressed!"

Although it wasn't really funny, laughter rippled around the conference table. That particular resident certainly had a way of getting right to the heart of the matter.

DECIDING TO HANG OUT my own shingle, to establish my own practice, was great fun. It meant I got to do all kind of things, like find and furnish an office, purchase all the medical and office equipment, and design all the systems I wanted to use. It was all up to me. I've always loved shopping and number-crunching, so the whole process was right up my alley. But the first thing I needed to do was obtain some money.

Before I went looking for financing, I got everything together I thought I would need. I began by closing my eyes and taking an imaginary tour of the office at the residency program where I had just finished my training, generating a list of all the equipment and supplies I would need. Next, I pored over medical supply catalogues, noting prices for all the items on my list. I created a fee schedule; then I projected how many patient visits I would have and how they would increase over time. After that I calculated how much income I could expect my new practice to generate, and how fast I could expect it. I combined those numbers with the shopping lists to decide how much up-front money I needed. Finally, I began calling the banks in my area. I was fully confident that as a medical professional (with a great personal credit rating to boot), I was a prime candidate for financing. Banks would be falling all over themselves, competing to lend me money!

Not.

One bank official stated over the phone that they wouldn't be interested in lending me any money unless the loan were fully collateralized. *If I had the collateral,* I thought, *I wouldn't need the loan.* As I hung up the phone, I thought to myself, *They are going to be so sorry they let a customer as wonderful as me get away.* It was confidence that served me well.

Next, I deposited the twins at daycare and packed the car with my three-month-old infant, his stroller, and a folder containing my projections and lists, and started making the rounds of the other banks in person. At the last minute,

I also slipped my previous year's tax return into the folder. I suddenly realized that I was going to look for all the world as if I wanted to open a savings account for my new baby. Boy, were those bankers going to be surprised when they heard I was a doctor looking for a loan to start my own practice!

I didn't get past the front desk in the first three banks I tried. I wasn't the least bit deterred, however; I was having fun. I walked into yet another bank. A short, chunky woman with finely coiffed graying hair greeted me, probably expecting to hear me say something about a savings account for the baby I was pushing ahead of me in the stroller.

"I'm a doctor, and I'm looking for a loan to start my own practice," I said.

She eyed me with an indeterminate expression.

"You don't have three years' tax returns with you, do you?" she asked.

"I have last year's return, plus projections for income and expenses for start-up and the first year of practice," I responded.

All she managed to say was, "Oh. Wait right here."

She went into the office of the branch manager, a slightly older woman, who returned in a moment and invited me into her office. We chatted for a while, and in short order she invited me to apply for a line of credit and produced the required application forms. She even held the baby while I filled them out on the spot.

That was fun. Being approved for the money to start the practice was even more fun.

I FOUND A LITTLE basement office about one block from the hospital. It had two exam rooms, a storage closet, a tiny lab area, a small office for me, and a waiting room. I signed the lease and began shopping in earnest: first, I needed furniture for the waiting room, exam rooms, and my office. I opened an account with a medical supply company and placed a large order from their catalogue. I opened for business the day the baby was five months old, and never looked back.

Finding and working with my staff was great fun. I hired a woman who had been working in medical offices for decades to be my receptionist, scheduler, and biller.

One day, after listening to someone on the phone for what seemed like forever, she hung up and burst into laughter.

"What's so funny?" I asked.

"The first words out of that woman's mouth were, 'I'm a no-nonsense kind of person,'" she gasped as she tried to contain her mirth.

"Yeah? So?"

"So then she proceeds to talk ten minutes of nonsense!"

Patients also had funny things to say.

One very pregnant woman came into the office wearing an attractive one-piece jumpsuit. I couldn't help myself;

I asked her, "How do you get out of that when you have to go to the bathroom?"

Her answer: "Very quickly!"

A nine-year-old boy visiting me for a checkup proved himself an expert conversationalist.

"Seen many broken bones today?" he asked out of the blue.

Sometimes I had to struggle to keep a straight face, like the time I asked a fifty-something woman about her family history.

"No; nothing unusual. I did have an uncle who dropped dead, but that's *normal.*"

I held my hand to my mouth as if muffling a sneeze, so she wouldn't see my struggle to remain respectful. I never did find out what was so normal about dropping dead.

Family practice obviously means I get to take care of families, but that designation doesn't refer to just parents and children. I have multiple three- and four-generation families in my practice at the moment, and it's always great fun to take care of them. Sometimes the strict rules of confidentiality go out the window, but only in families who have expressly told me that they don't mind. Often, they call ahead of time to let me know about things they are afraid a family member won't tell me. Other times I don't find out until later.

I saw one man with a swollen leg and shortness of breath who'd been having problems for two days; or so he said. I was worried that he had a blood clot in his lungs, so I advised him to go to the hospital right away. I didn't want him to drive, so I called his sister to come and pick him up. She, her husband, and their children were all my patients. So were the man's other sister and that sister's husband and children; and the three siblings' parents, at least until their father's death a few years ago. I still see their mother. This is a family that shares everything. The patient knew it, and he knew what his sister was going to say when she came to get him: "Does he have a blood clot?"

"Yes," I said. "I think so."

"We told him to call you two weeks ago!"

The patient didn't mind. Luckily he did well, despite the blood clots in his legs and lungs.

Over the years, I've found that not only have I been taking care of families, but my practice has also extended to taking care of other, larger groups of people. Many families find doctors via recommendations from people they know. This means that when satisfied patients tell their friends about me, I wind up taking care of neighborhoods, play-groups, and classrooms.

In my office is a bulletin board that holds pictures of my patients; the photos are usually of children, given to me by their parents. Once a picture goes up, it doesn't often come down. It may get covered with an updated picture of the same child, but I have to admit that there are baby pictures up there of children who are now well past infancy.

One day a fourth-grade girl was staring at a picture of a toddler on my bulletin board. As her mother walked over, the child pointed to the picture and said, "That looks just like a girl in my class!" I smiled. Her classmate was also my patient, and the picture she had noticed was in fact that child's baby picture.

That was fun.

B ACK WHEN I WAS a medical student, I once had the opportunity to listen to long-time family doctor Warren B. Matthews—who was younger then than I am now— expound on the advantages of solo practice. One thing he said about his patients stuck with me. He pointed out that in a solo practice, you eventually wind up treating people you like, who like you.

After nearly two decades in practice myself, I can report that this is absolutely true. And it is what makes life one helluva lot of fun.

# Half of what is taught in medical school is wrong, but no one knows which half.

"MEDICAL SCHOOL graduates, honored guests, ladies and gentlemen, welcome to this year's graduation ceremony. I know you all join me in wishing the best to these new physicians as they begin their distinguished careers, and I hope you will indulge me as I share some time-honored wisdom with them today.

"It's been four years since you came to us. Four long years. Probably the four most expensive years of your education."

(Appreciative chuckles from the audience; perhaps a little more restrained in the parents' section.)

"Certainly they have been four of the most intellectually and emotionally challenging years of your life. All of those lectures, quizzes, tests, and exams covering so much material. Biochemistry; physiology; anatomy; histology; pathology; pharmacology; the list goes on and on."

(A whisper from the students' section: *"I'm afraid he will, too."*)

"Medical school as we know it today is a relatively recent development in the education and training of physicians. Three hundred years ago, one learned to become a physician in this country by apprenticing oneself to a doctor already in practice. By following him around, watching as he practiced his art, and hopefully availing yourself of whatever teaching he was willing and able to offer, medical knowledge was passed along from one generation to another. As with all apprenticeships, though, education is limited to the knowledge possessed by the master with whom one chooses to apprentice, and his willingness to share it."

(Another whisper: *"Oh, no! There's no stopping him now."*)

"Medical education was different in Europe, where the accepted venue for medical training was the university and its affiliated teaching hospital. Many Americans went abroad to study, although the process was arduous. Because of this, though, only the most qualified students stuck it out and were then able to return home with substantial medical knowledge to share. This public dissemination was accomplished as early as 1750 with public lectures on various medical topics, primarily in Philadelphia, then the epicenter of American medicine. By 1765 the first formal American medical school was founded by the College of Philadelphia, in conjunction with the Pennsylvania Hospital. Thus the classical model of a medical school as an intrinsic part of an institution of higher education with an affiliation with a public hospital rose in the New World.

"Over the next century, though, numerous proprietary medical schools—schools run mainly for profit, by doctors of questionable qualifications—arose throughout the country. Many schools required only the payment of tuition and fees for graduation..."

(*"Hah! I guess some things never change."*
*"Shush."*)

"...and were affiliated with neither a college or university nor a hospital. Because medicine was not yet considered a scientific endeavor, different medical sects arose, each with its own belief system about health and disease. The homeopaths, the osteopaths, the allopaths, the naturopaths, the eclectics, and the physiomedicals, among others, each began with a preconceived notion about the nature of the human body and its response to disease, from which arose various paradigms for treatment. Many of these sects founded their own schools, with their own varying standards for admission and graduation. The diagnosis and treatment you received as a patient, not to mention the education available to you as a student or an apprentice, depended entirely on which paradigm you happened to encounter, and whose disciple was teaching or treating you."

*("So back then, it was all sects education."*

*"Shut up already.")*

"By the end of the 19th century, modern medicine finally emerged as a primarily science-based discipline. At the beginning of the 20th century, Abraham Flexner—interestingly, not a physician but an educator—generated his famous report, 'Medical Education in the United States and Canada.' More than any other document, the Flexner Report shaped medical education into what it is today: a prerequisite background with emphasis in the basic sciences, followed by a two-year course in the basic medical sciences, followed by two years of clinical training at the bedsides of actual patients."

*("So from the very beginning we had non-doctors in charge of educating doctors."*

*"Will you shut up!")*

"As medicine became recognized as a science, the scientific method—with all its pros and cons—became the means by which medicine advanced.

"Science is neither easy nor quick; witness how many centuries it took for general acceptance of the idea that the earth revolves around the sun. All the basic concepts we hold today about how the universe works, from chemistry's periodic table to the physiology of the circulatory system, have been painstakingly derived from the scientific method of observation, hypothesis, experimentation, and confirmation. This process is slow and unsteady. Cherished theories are frequently found wanting and need to be discarded, and the process must begin anew. Science has seen plenty of false starts and dead-ends through the millennia."

("As opposed to his speeches, which are full of false ends and dead starts."

"If you don't shut up, you're next year's rectal exam volunteer for the whole class.")

"For example, there was a time when it was accepted that life arose spontaneously; that living things could arise from non-living matter. This theory came from the observation that when bread and rags were left in a box outdoors overnight, mice were present in the morning. It seemed obvious that the rodents had arisen spontaneously from raw materials that just happened to serve as their food and shelter. Even after the development of the microscope and the identification of bacteria—germs too small to be seen with the naked eye—the idea of spontaneous generation was still considered valid: broth left out in the open could found teeming with microorganisms in short order. It took more rigorous scientific thinking to imagine that the bread and rags were attracting rodents from elsewhere in the universe instead of actually causing them to be generated de novo, or that airborne germs might be responsible for spoiling the broth. Eventually, Louis Pasteur definitively disproved the concept of spontaneous generation with his demonstration that broth in a swan-necked flask—a glass container designed to prevent airborne contamination—remained completely free of life."

("*Just like this speech.*"

"*Dude! No gloves for you!*"

"*Will someone please stifle that guy?*")

"Because we seem to have come so far in our understanding of the workings of the universe and the human body, it is sometimes difficult to conceive of all that we don't yet know. Therefore, if there is only one thing you take away from this speech today, let it be this: half of what we have taught you in medical school is wrong, but no one knows which half."

("*Great. What are we supposed to do now?*")

FIVE YEARS LATER, sitting around together drinking beer at a medical-school class reunion:

"Guess what, everyone! I found out that the sight of blood makes me faint, so I went back to graduate school for a doctorate. Now I'm doing medical research."

"Cool! So you're the one in charge of finding out which half of what they taught us in medical school was wrong."

"Whoa, dudes, you know it's not that simple. We can't actually prove that something was wrong based on just one experiment or a couple of studies. Science doesn't work like that. It takes a long time. You have to do the same studies over and over to prove anything definitively. You have to be patient."

"So what do we do in the meantime?"

"The same thing we've been doing all along: assume everything they taught us was right."

"How much proof do we have to wait for?"

"That's up to you."

"What do you mean by that?"

"Out in your office-based practice, no one tells you what to do. You can read the literature and talk to other doctors and find out for yourself what the science says. Some of you are harder to convince than others, and you all incorporate changes into your practice at different rates. It can be a long, drawn-out process to admit that something they taught us in medical school was wrong."

FIVE YEARS AFTER THAT, sitting around together drinking white wine at another medical-school class reunion:

"Hey, here comes Dr. Olympus!"

"Why do you call him that? He's not a surgeon who thinks he's an old-time Greek god. He's a gastroenterologist who spends all his time doing endoscopies of assorted orifices."

"Exactly. Olympus is thinking of naming their next colonoscope model after him."

"Hey, Scopes; what's new?"

"We found out something they taught in med school that was wrong."

"Really! Do tell."

"Remember how we were taught that ulcers were just caused by stomach acid?"

"Yeah. I'll never forget the old saying, 'No acid, no ulcer.' That's why it was so cool when they finally came up with drugs that actually cut the production of stomach acid. We actually have effective medicine instead of just settling for antacids to neutralize it. Why? Did people start getting ulcers without acid?"

"No, but didn't you notice that the ulcers kept coming back? We figured it was stress. If only there were some way to get those Type A personalities to rest, relax, and mend their driven ways, their ulcers would be gone for good. But back in 1982, a couple of docs in Australia found a bacterium that lives in the stomach."

"No way! The pH of the stomach is between 1 and 2. It's impossible for any bacteria to live in an environment that acidic."

"Well, it did. It was spiral-shaped, so they named it *Helicobacter pylori.*"

"Why?"

"From the Latin. 'Helix' means 'spiral.' And 'pylori.' Like the round muscle at the end of the stomach, the pylorus, right before the duodenum. Don't you remember anything from anatomy?"

A deliberate sip of chardonnay.

"How did they find out it had anything to do with ulcers?"

"They went all the way back to the very beginning of microbiology and used Koch's postulates."

"Now I know you're pulling our leg, dude. To do that, they'd have to find the bug in people with ulcers but not in people without them. Then they'd have to isolate it, grow it in a pure culture and re-introduce it into someone who was healthy who then got sick. Then, just for good measure, they'd have to re-isolate it from the poor schmuck they gave it to and determine that it was still the same germ."

"Actually, they figured that if they eradicated the germ with antibiotics—which they could prove with endoscopy…"

"Any excuse to pass a scope!"

"As I was saying, they realized that the logical equivalent of passing the bacterium to an uninfected host and observing for the development of disease would be getting rid of the bacteria and observing that the ulcers didn't come back. Even so, it turns out one of the Australian guys actually did it!"

"What? He infected himself with *H. pylori?*"

"Yep. Came down with ulcers, too."

"Jeez. He was either dedicated or crazy."

"Probably both. Let's drink to Dr. Robin Warren and Dr. Barry Marshall."

"Which was which?"

"Dr. Warren was dedicated; Dr. Marshall was the crazy one."

Glasses clink.

"Something they taught us in medical school proven wrong. One down, another 49 percent to go."

A NOTHER FIVE YEARS LATER, sitting around together drinking red wine at the next medical-school class reunion:

"Dr. Cards! How goes the heart business?"

"Fine, fine. Keeping busy. Everyone has a heart and they all want to keep it beating. So I'll never starve."

"Yeah, not the way you guys order every test imaginable on every patient."

"Quit muttering. No one told you to go into family practice."

"Oh, I'm not complaining. I love what I do. It just gets frustrating when I tell all my patients to stop smoking, watch their diet, exercise regularly, and lose weight, only to have them come back from their visit with you saying, 'The cardiologist said I have to stop smoking, watch my diet, exercise regularly, and lose weight, so I guess I'd better.' I feel like a broken record that no one's listening to in the first place."

"Don't worry, Marcus. Your patients love you. They just come to me for prescriptions."

"News flash, Dr. Heart God; I have a prescription pad, too. And I know how to use it. I measure cholesterol and I diagnose diabetes, which, as you know, are the major risk factors for heart attacks and strokes. I prescribe cholesterol-lowering medicines for everyone at high risk for coronary artery disease, and beta-blockers for patients with congestive heart failure."

"What!?! You can't give beta-blockers to patients with congestive heart failure! Don't you remember the sympathetic nervous system? The fight-or-flight response is what speeds up the heart and raises the blood pressure. Adrenaline triggers that response. Don't you remember anything about the alpha and beta receptors it stimulates? If you block those, especially the beta receptors in the heart, the heart will slow down and not beat as hard. In congestive heart failure, the heart is already having trouble keeping up with the forward flow of blood. That's why the blood backs up into the lungs, which is what makes the patient short of breath."

"Haven't you been reading your own clinical literature? They found that small doses of beta-blockers decrease the blood pressure in the aorta and systemic circulation more than they decrease the strength of the heart's contraction. So the net effect is positive and the patients feel better. They also live longer." (Takes a triumphant swig of merlot.)

"You know, I thought I saw something like that in a journal last month, but I've been so busy in the cath lab that I haven't had the chance to read up on it."

"Well then, it's a good thing you have me to tell you about it, isn't it?"

"One more thing they taught us in medical school proven wrong!"

FIVE MORE YEARS GO BY, sitting around together drinking shots at the next medical-school class reunion:

"Hey, Dr. Alan; we should call you Al, now that you're a pulmonologist. You know; short for 'alveoli.'"

"Cute."

"So how's it going in the land of the lungs?"

"Well, my practice is going fine, but I lost a ton of money in the stock market."

"Oh, no! How come?"

"Asthma."

"Asthma? What does asthma have to do with the stock market?"

"Remember how we were taught that asthma was mainly caused by airway constriction, when the smooth muscle fibers around the little bronchioles constrict and squeeze the passages almost shut? That's what makes the musical wheezing noises we hear when we listen to the chest of someone having an asthma attack. Those muscle fibers are controlled by the sympathetic nervous system, so we can get them to relax by having the patient inhale a drug that works like adrenaline. The muscles loosen, the airways open, and the patient can breathe again."

"We all know that. What does that have to do with the stock market? Did you buy up stock in all the companies making the inhalers?"

"No, I bought the companies making theophylline."

"What?"

"You remember theophylline. It's a chemical cousin of caffeine and it also relaxes the smooth muscle around the airways."

"I know all about theophylline. I hate prescribing it. I know you can give it either orally or intravenously, but it causes nausea, vomiting, and seizures if the dose is too high."

"Yes, but if you monitor the blood levels carefully the patients are usually okay."

"So what's the problem with theophylline?"

"It used to be made in lots of different formulations by a bunch of different manufacturers. It was a real pain keeping track of which ones were interchangeable and how a given patient reacted to them. Then this start-up company developed a new formulation that they swore would work exactly the same in every patient every single time. As a pulmonologist treating lots of people with asthma, I figured I could clean up if I bought stock in this company and then switched all my patients onto their new drug as soon as it came out."

"Sounds like a good plan. What happened?"

"The literature began reporting studies about the role of airway inflammation in asthma. The lining of the airways secretes more mucus in response to things like allergy, infection, and tobacco smoke. The inflammatory response produces swelling in the airways that narrows the lumen and thickens the walls."

"Schmutz in the pipes."

"What, Marcus?"

"I've read about this too. I call it 'schmutz in the pipes' when I explain it to patients."

"Oh. Well, back when I was in training, only the patients sick enough to present to the emergency room got treated with anti-inflammatory drugs like steroids. We thought they were only necessary in severe cases. But now, as we come to understand asthma better, we've begun treating many more patients with inhaled steroids."

"What about theophylline?"

"I can't remember the last time I wrote a prescription for it. The drug company whose stock I bought went belly-up. Now I have to start saving for retirement all over again." (Tosses back another shot.)

"Just goes to show you; there's something *else* they taught us in medical school that turned out to be wrong."

FIVE YEARS AFTER THAT, sitting around together drinking cocktails at the next medical-school class reunion:

"Hey, Dr. Cooper! They finally let you out of the operating room long enough to join us. What's new in the world of surgery?"

"Not much. Same old, same old. Nothing ever changes."

"What are you talking about? I just read a review article about the treatment of breast cancer and how dramatically it's changed over the last 50 years."

"Well, I guess so."

"You guess so? My God, man, at the beginning of the 20th century most women thought breast cancer was a death sentence, mainly because it was. Doctors couldn't do much for it, so women just sat at home and watched while lumps in their breasts grew, spread under their arms, broke through the skin, spread everywhere else, and killed them. It wasn't pretty."

"Well, yeah. But William Halstead changed all that."

"Yeah, by popularizing the radical mastectomy—massive surgery to remove the breast, all the lymph nodes under the arm, and the muscles of the chest wall all the way down to the rib cage."

"Well, yeah, but back then they thought that tumors spread just by growing bigger and bigger, so the more tissue they removed, the more likely they were to get it all out and the less likely the woman was to die from the disease. It may have been disfiguring, but it was considered the only option."

"I'll give you that. Halstead did offer a viable treatment option. So doctors worked to get the message out to women that early detection of breast cancer could now reduce the chance of dying from it, even though they didn't actually have any proof of that statement without cancer registries and tumor boards to track patients' responses to treatment and how the patients eventually ended up. Still, they were successful enough that there were lots of radical mastectomies performed."

Pause for another sip of martini.

"By the 1950s, some surgeons began to have doubts. The public relations program had been so successful at getting women to come in when they first discovered lumps in their breasts that surgeons were now dealing with smaller tumors in much earlier stages of the disease. The first long-term studies were also beginning to show that the survival benefit of the radical mastectomy might not be as great as originally thought. But no one had the balls to challenge the great William Halstead until a doctor named George Crile, Jr., came along. He suggested removing just the breast while leaving the chest-wall muscles and the large block of tissues in the armpit."

"Yeah, and then his own wife was diagnosed with breast cancer. She had just the simple mastectomy instead of the radical surgery, and the cancer spread to her brain and ended up killing her. You can just imagine how horrified his colleagues were!"

"He stuck to his guns, though, and by the 1970s other surgeons were experimenting with procedures that removed even less tissue, trying to cut out only the cancerous lump itself. Believe it or not, Dr. Crile's second wife also developed breast cancer and had a lumpectomy. She survived!"

"Yeah, but you forgot that by this time, there were lots of new chemotherapy drugs that could kill cancer cells throughout the body. They were also developing radiation therapy to get rid of any malignant cells remaining in the breast after surgery. It was pretty complicated to sort out what combination of treatments would be most effective for any given patient."

"But by the 1980s there were enough studies with enough patients to show that lumpectomy plus radiation produced the same survival rates as mastectomy. Even now, we're coming to understand more and more about the genetics of specific tumors, and we're developing newer, more targeted treatments than ever before."

"So what you're saying is that in the final analysis, it took about 50 years to prove that something else we were taught in medical school was wrong."

FIVE YEARS LATER, sitting around together drinking umbrella drinks at the next medical-school class reunion:

"Hey, guys; remember all those years ago when that blowhard at graduation claimed that half of what they taught us in medical school was wrong, but they don't know which half?"

"Yeah. What about it?"

"Over the years we've found about out all kinds of things we learned that we now know were wrong, like the patho-physiology of stomach ulcers and asthma, and the treatment of breast cancer."

"Yeah. So?"

"So much else has changed as well. But according to

our graduation speaker, half of what they taught us has been right all along. Can you think of anything they taught us that hasn't changed after all this time?"

"Absolutely!"

"Oh yeah, Nelson; like what?"

"We spent a lot of time in pediatrics talking about immunizations. By the time we graduated, we could already protect children against polio, diphtheria, tetanus, pertussis, measles, mumps, and rubella. Just since then we've added hepatitis, pneumococcal disease, meningitis, chickenpox, and rotavirus, with more on the way. Even though there are crazy people out there trying to get patients to believe that vaccines cause autism, every study we do continues to reinforce the safety and efficacy of childhood immunization. One of the greatest medical advances of all time has to be the elimination of vaccine-preventable diseases of childhood."

"I can agree with that. We've already eradicated smallpox from the entire world, and we have the ability to get rid of polio as well. All that's stopping us is the sociopolitical issues of the developing world."

"You mean Africa is all messed up."

"Right."

"Okay, that's one thing. Anyone else? Litman? Did they get anything right about cardiology?"

"Well, yeah, actually they did."

"Oh?"

"I had a student in my office last week for his cardiology rotation. We were going over EKGs and he showed me the book he was using to learn how to read them. Guys, it was exactly the same book *we* used."

"Really? Wasn't it a new edition at least?"

"Well, yes, but I looked through it and there were really no substantive differences that I could see. The electricity running though the heart doesn't change over time. Sure, now we have a zillion more ways to treat different kinds of heart disease, as well as newer ways to diagnose it. Heaven knows we're taking people to the cath lab at the drop of a hat compared to back when we graduated. But the EKG hasn't changed. Reading it hasn't changed, and learning to read it hasn't changed. I would say they got that one right, too."

"Okay then. That's another. More, anyone?"

"Everything they taught us about how bad smoking is was right on target."

"That's true. How many cancers has smoking been associated with?"

"Lung. Esophagus. Head and neck."

"Now we also know about kidney, bladder, and cervical cancer."

"Isn't it also a co-factor for skin cancer?"

"Probably."

"Okay; what other diseases are caused or exacerbated by smoking?"

"Heart disease. Asthma. Chronic obstructive lung disease."

"Anything else?"

"Allergies."

"Has anything positive been discovered about smoking, even after all this time?"

"Nope."

"Has any study ever disproved any of smoking's adverse effects?"

"No."

"So I suppose everyone can agree that everything we learned in medical school about the use and abuse of tobacco was right?"

"Dead on."

"Bad pun. Next round's on you."

"Deal."

"What were we talking about?"

"Things we learned in med school that were right."

"Oh, yeah."

"Well? Was there anything else?"

"Yes, indeed."

"Andre, dude. Good to see you. What else did the old farts at med school get right?"

"As you all know, I went into orthopedics. And it turns out that the basic principles of fracture healing haven't changed since long before we graduated. Do whatever it takes to get the broken ends of the bone next to each other in the best approximation of anatomic alignment that you can, and stabilize them. Whether that means an operation—complete with pins, plates, and screws—or just a simple cast depends on the characteristics of the specific fracture. Then let the osteoblasts do their thing and make new bone, knitting the pieces back into one. The osteoclasts will break it down, and between the actions of the two kinds of cells the new bone will remodel itself until it's a perfect replica of the original."

"That's pretty cool, Andre. I forget; how long does it take for a bone to heal?"

"Usually about six to eight weeks, though of course it varies depending on the bone, how far apart the fragments are, and the patient's age and general health. As a rule, kids heal up really quickly. One of my attendings once told me that in a kid, if the ends of the bone are in the same room they'll heal up just fine."

"Okay, then. The score is tied. Things they taught us that were wrong include the cause of stomach ulcers, the use of beta-blockers in heart disease, the pathophysiology of asthma, and the optimal treatment of breast cancer. Things they got right are immunizations against vaccine-preventable diseases, how to read an EKG, smoking is bad, and how bones heal. That's four of each. Anyone want to break the tie?"

"I can."

"Marcus! Glad you could tear yourself away from your luxurious solo office to join us."

"I didn't get very far. I'm still on call."

"You were going to break the tie?"

"Oh, yes. Do you remember what they told us at the very beginning of our course on interviewing the patient and physical diagnosis?"

"Um, they said a lot. What exactly are you talking about?"

"They quoted the Oath of Maimonides."

"I don't remember that. Who's Maimonides?"

"He was a medieval physician and rabbi who wrote his own medical oath. I wanted us to recite it at graduation, but I was outvoted. We ended up taking the modern version of the Hippocratic oath."

"Nothing wrong with Hippocrates, dude."

"Nothing wrong with him, but his oath is terribly outdated, despite all the different attempts to 'update' it. Do you realize that according to the real Hippocratic oath, we're not supposed to share our teachings with anyone? That means that patient education is outlawed."

"No one interprets it that way anymore."

"True. But did you know that it also says we're supposed to revere our teachers, including providing for them in their old age?"

Eruption of generalized laughter.

"With all the tuition money they got from me, they can damn well fund their own retirements!"

"So what was so memorable about the Oath of Maimonides, Marcus?"

"We were all giggling nervously about dealing with patients; snickering about seeing them naked, and stuff like that. Then the professor quoted this line: 'May I never see in the patient anything other than a fellow creature in pain.' That shut me right up."

"Yeah; now I think I remember that, too. But what does that have to do with stuff they got right, Marcus?"

"Just this. What was the first thing they taught us about interviewing patients? Don't interrupt. Let the patient have his say, because 90 percent of the time, the patient will tell you what is wrong with him. I have to admit that the longer I do family practice, I think it's much higher than that; higher than 99 percent, most likely."

"So they were right when they told us to listen to patients."

"More than that. Everything about treating the patient instead of just treating the disease; everything about the emotional aspects of illness; everything about making a personal connection with our patients, because at the end of it all, when we have no more surgery or medicine or treatments left to offer them, all we have is ourselves. That's what makes it all worthwhile.

"They were right about that."

## NINTH LAW

# Poor planning on your part does not constitute an emergency on my part.

**T**HE PHONE RINGS in the middle of the night.

"Hello?"

"Doctor, I need to make an appointment with you right away."

"Are you having a medical emergency? Chest pain? Severe bleeding? Trouble breathing? Can't see/hear/speak? Can't move an arm or leg? Convulsions?"

"No. I just need to make an appointment to see you."

"What's the problem?"

"I can't sleep."

*Wonderful*, I think. *Now that makes two of us.*

I stifle a yawn. "How about if you call the office in the morning. We'll be happy to make the appointment for you then."

"Okay, Doctor. Thank you very much."

I know how he feels. I need my goddamned sleep.

TIME AND SPACE are funny things. In the grand scheme of the universe both are infinite, yet our limited human life span demands that each must have boundaries. Just as we build fences around our yards and hedges around our fields to delineate our space on this earth, humans have found ways to divide our lives into units we call time; the better to manage all the things we find ourselves doing as we make our way from the cradle to the grave.

Luckily, we have a planet that rotates as it circles its sun, conveniently dividing time into night and day. Probably not coincidentally, our bodies have evolved so as to require a certain proportion of "down time" to recover from the demands of the activities of life. Thus, we have the arbitrary division of time into days—corresponding to a single rotation of the planet—divided approximately into half, during which both activity and recovery typically occur.

Like most diurnal mammals, I work during the day and I sleep at night. I work hard, taking care of my patients in the office, in the hospital, and at their homes; and then I come home to rest, relax, and re-charge myself for the day to come. If I do not get enough sleep, I—like all other animals who do not get enough sleep—will not function optimally.

I need my goddamned sleep.

I understand completely that my calling of solo family practice includes the obligation to be available to my patients 24 hours a day. Other doctors share call; I do not. I am also ready, willing, and able to respond to my patients' legitimate needs whenever they may arise. But there are limits.

I need my goddamned sleep.

IN THE OFFICE the morning after that phone call, I struggle through the day. That's what happens when I don't get enough sleep.

I check the appointment book to see if my middle-of-the-night patient has called for an appointment yet. I do not see his name. Finally, at the end of the day, I ask my secretary to call him in order to schedule. I understand that insomnia can be a real problem, and by now I am feeling sorry for the patient and his sleeping problems. Also, I am unwilling to take the risk that he will call me again in the wee hours.

I hear her on the phone with him. She hangs up. She has not picked up her pencil or flipped through the appointment book to find him an open slot. These are not good signs.

"He yelled at me," she reports.

"Why? *He* called *me* in the middle of the night complaining that he couldn't sleep. Not getting enough sleep can be a serious problem, so he ought to come for us to evaluate him. I asked him to call us, but I thought it would be polite if we called him instead. Why did he yell at you?"

"I woke him up."

"Oh. I guess he's not having any trouble sleeping anymore."

Things should only be that simple.

The phone rings again in the middle of the night.

"Doctor, I can't sleep again. I need to see you."

"How long have you had this problem?"

"Just since last night."

"Sir, the reason you're having trouble sleeping right now is because you were asleep at 4:00 P.M. when my secretary called to offer you an office appointment."

"So?"

"It's important to keep regular hours for sleep. You should also avoid caffeine, exercise, and heavy meals within several hours of going to bed. You should keep your bedroom dark, quiet, and cool, and you shouldn't do anything in bed except sleep. There could also be a physical or emotional problem interfering with sleep, so you ought to make an appointment with me at the office, *during the daytime*, to evaluate your problem."

"So what should I do now?"

"Call the office in the morning and make an appointment."

"I mean, what should I do right now, while I can't sleep?"

Slowly, silently, I count to ten. Then twenty. Whatever happens, I must not utter the words shrieking through my brain like a psychotic banshee on steroids, which are, "*I really don't give a flying rat's patootie!*"

"Please just call the office in the morning. Good night."

For the second night in a row, I am not getting my goddamned sleep.

For the second day in a row, I am cranky at the office. For the second day in a row I search in vain for the patient's name in the appointment book. For the second day in a row, I insist that my secretary call the patient again.

I watch as she gets him on the phone. I listen to what appears to be an animated conversation. I hold my breath as she lifts her pencil. I exhale sharply as she puts it down again without having written anything in the appointment book. I walk over to her as she hangs up the phone.

"He says thanks for the advice about avoiding caffeine and exercise before bed, and keeping the room cool and dark. He's been drinking coffee after his evening workout, and leaving the television on while he's trying to sleep. He said he'd stop doing that."

"Good. I hope it works."

"So does he. He said he'd call you if he had any more problems."

I can only hope he does so during the day. I need my goddamned sleep.

THE PHONE RINGS one night as I am preparing dinner. "Hello?"

"Doctor, I need a refill on my prescriptions."

"Now?"

"Yes."

"What drugs do you take?"

"Don't you know? You're my doctor."

"Mrs. White, all of your medications are written down in your chart at my office. I'm not at my office right now. What does it say on your pill bottles?"

"I don't know where the bottles are."

"Then how do you know you need refills?"

"Because I just remembered that the last time I filled them, the nice pharmacist told me that there weren't any refills and I should call you to refill them."

"Why don't you call the office tomorrow and we can get it all straightened out for you."

"Okay, Doctor. Thank you."

"You're welcome, Mrs. White."

As I hang up the phone, a thought comes to me and I grab the receiver back, hoping against hope that she hasn't hung up yet.

"Mrs. White!" No luck; she's gone.

If she can't find her pill bottles, how is she going to take her medications?

THE PHONE RINGS just as I am sitting down to dinner.

"Hello?"

"Doctor, I need a refill on my prescriptions."

"Now?"

"Yes, I'm all out of pills."

"What pills do you take?"

"Well, there's two for my blood pressure, one for my diabetes, one for my cholesterol, and that inhaler you gave me for my asthma."

"How long have you been out of them?"

"Three weeks."

I want to ask why he needs them at this specific moment, as opposed to, say, tomorrow morning, when I am in the office with access to his chart, which will tell me when he was last in the office and when he is due for blood work to monitor his diabetes and cholesterol. But I don't, because I want to get back to my dinner.

"In that case, why don't you call the office in the morning and we can get you scheduled for a checkup as well."

"Okay, Doctor."

THE PHONE RINGS in the middle of dinner.

"Hello?"

"Doctor, I need a refill on my prescriptions."

"Now?"

"Yes. I'm down to one refill."

"Then you still have a refill and you don't need them now."

"Oh. I guess not."

"Please call the office during regular hours tomorrow and we'll get you squared away."

"Thanks."

THE PHONE RINGS one evening as I am cleaning up after a dinner party.

"Hello?"

"Doctor, I need a refill on my prescriptions."

"Right now?"

"Yes, I don't have any left for tomorrow."

"But the pharmacy isn't open now, and I'm going to be in the office first thing in the morning. Can it wait until I get there so I can pull your chart?"

"Sure."

THE PHONE RINGS one Saturday afternoon just as I am sitting down to lunch.

"Hello?"

"Doctor, I need a refill on the antibiotic you wrote for my baby's ear infection."

"But I gave you just enough medicine to take care of the problem. The baby shouldn't need any more of it."

"But she knocked the bottle over."

"Ah. Of course. Kids do that all the time. Let me see; when did I see her in the office?"

"Monday."

"Okay. Today is Saturday, so she should be halfway through the ten-day course of medication. So I'll call you in another half a bottle and that should hold you."

"But she spilled it on Wednesday."

The metallic taste of blood stings my mouth as I bite down—hard—on my own tongue. It's the only way I can avoid shrieking like a psychotic wolf howling at the moon, *"Then why the* hell *did you wait until today to call?"*

"What pharmacy do you use?" I ask instead.

Damn, I'm good; even when I don't want to be.


I AM ONLY HUMAN, and as such I have bodily needs. In addition to sleep, I require food (aside from chunks of my own tongue) to sustain my body. This is necessary in order to provide my patients with the thorough, dutiful care that they expect. I understand that the obligation I have taken on in treating them includes making certain that they have the life-preserving medications that I prescribe. But why oh why do they always call while I'm trying to eat? Or while I'm sleeping! I need my goddamned sleep too.

THE ULTIMATE CALL for prescription refills:

"Doctor, I'm all out of my medicines. I don't have the bottles, I don't know what pharmacy I use, and my car won't start."

Through the years, I have learned how not to say things. As such, I have developed my own personal code. When the words that come out of my mouth are, "How can I help you?" it means that the words shrieking through my head like the roar of a psychotic jet overhead are, "What the hell do you want *me* to do about it?"

MY OFFICE HOURS are by appointment. This is the best arrangement I can come up with to make the best use of both my patients' time and mine.

If I had no set appointments but rather allowed patients to come in whenever they wanted, and saw them on a first-come, first-served basis, it would be efficient for me but not for my patients, who would never know how long they might have to wait to see me. With the advance arrangement of a mutually agreeable time, both the patient and I can go about our business until the appointed moment for our encounter. Assuming everyone does their part, patients by showing up on time and me by staying on schedule (which, unlike the negative stereotype of a physician, I usually manage to do quite well, thank you), everyone is happy.

In order for this system to work, though, patients have to do their part.

"Hello, I'd like to make an appointment to see the doctor right away. This is Mrs. Green."

My secretary responds, "I can help you with that. What kind of problem are you having?"

"I'd rather not say."

"Well, Mrs. Green, in order to make an appointment for you we need to know approximately how much time the doctor will need to take care of you. To do that, we need to have some idea of what's wrong."

"Can't you just say it's personal?"

"Can you give me some idea of how long it's been going on?"

"Oh, it's been a while."

"A long while? A short while?"

"Oh, quite a while."

There are times when making an appointment is almost as challenging as getting the medical history.

"Okay, Mrs. Green, can you come in at 10:00 A.M.?"

"Ten? No, I'm at work and I have a meeting I can't possibly miss. Do you have any other time?"

"Sure; how about eleven?"

"Oh, no. I have a conference call then."

"Twelve?"

"No, there's a client coming in then."

"Later this afternoon?"

"No, I have too much paperwork to catch up on."

"How about sometime tomorrow?"

"But I can't wait until tomorrow!"

What would Marcus Welby do?

BY AND LARGE, I'm pretty good at accommodating urgent appointments. Unfortunately, I am often reminded that poor planning on your part does not constitute an emergency on my part.

"This is Mrs. Brown. I have to see the doctor right now!"

"Okay, come right over. How long will it take you to get here?"

"Let me see. I have to shower, walk the dog, and feed the cats. Then I have to go over to the school and drop off my son's book report that he forgot this morning. After I stop off and get some coffee, I should be there in about an hour and a half."

Three hours later, the patient arrives.

"Hello, Mrs. Brown. What seems to be the problem today?"

"I have this rash on my arm."

"Does it itch or hurt?"

"No."

"How long have you had it?"

"About six months."

"Have you tried anything for it?"

"Well, no. I didn't know what it was."

I peer at skin as clear and smooth as a baby's buttock.

"Um, I'm sorry; where is the rash?"

The patient looks at the arm she has been extending to me and exclaims, "Oh, I'm sorry. It's the other arm." The first sleeve is pulled back down while the other is pushed up, revealing skin as clear and smooth as a baby's other buttock.

"I'm sorry, Mrs. Brown, but I can't see anything on your skin."

The patient takes her other hand and rubs the area vigorously.

"Hang on a minute. I'm sure it was here somewhere."

I inspect the area again; still no rash to be seen.

"Good news, Mrs. Brown; it seems to have gotten better."

"Oh, okay then. I suppose I'll just have to wait until my appointment at the dermatologist this afternoon."

"You're seeing the dermatologist today?"

"Yes, at three o'clock. You have no idea how long I had to wait to get that appointment!"

MANY THINGS IN LIFE require appointments. The urgency of the need for an appointment is often inversely proportional to how easily that appointment is obtained. If you want your hair prepared in a stunning up-do for the prom, you'd better make sure you have it scheduled well in advance, lest you find your hairdresser fully booked by the time the prom actually rolls around. Other appointment-requiring encounters can be more forgiving. The difference between getting the dog groomed this week versus next week is rarely life-altering. Doctors' appointments tend to fall somewhere between the extremes. With my "open-access" scheduling policy, I am able to accommodate most requests for same-day appointments. Many other specialists are not.

"Thank you for calling the Pediatric Development Clinic. How can I help you?"

"My child is having a lot of trouble in school. He's in danger of failing, and I was told to call to make an appointment for an evaluation."

"We specialize in school issues, so we can certainly help you with that. Let's see; the first appointment we have available is in August."

"But this is October."

"I'm sorry, but we're very busy."

"How can you help keep him from failing school this year if you can't even see him until the school year is over?"

"Look, do you want the appointment or not?"

Sadly, this is a true story.

"I HURT MYSELF. I have to see the doctor right away!"

"Hi, Mr. Gray. What seems to be the problem?"

"I hurt my toe."

"How did you do that?"

"I dropped a hammer on it."

"When?"

"Two weeks ago."

Mr. Gray comes in, and I inspect the nail of the toe that he indicates. It is rough, thickened, and yellowed. I can see no signs of bleeding or bruising. I press on it lightly and watch as he fails to flinch. The rough, thickened, yellow appearance is consistent with chronic fungal infection of the nail that cannot possibly have developed over merely the last two weeks. Its appearance is more consistent with about three years of infection.

"How long has the nail looked rough and yellow like that?"

"About three years."

Damn, I'm good.

"That looks like a fungal infection of the nail, Mr. Gray. Nothing to worry about. So what happened when you dropped the hammer on it?"

"It hurt."

"And what did you do?"

"I put some ice on it and took some painkillers."

"So far, so good. Does is still hurt?"

"Not really."

I continue to stare at the proffered toe, nodding as if thinking deep thoughts about a puzzling clinical presentation, although the most puzzling aspect of this particular clinical presentation is what the hell the patient is doing here. What I'm really trying to do is come up with a tactful way of finding out what the hell the patient is doing here.

Got it!

"How can I help you?" It's a fantastic, all-purpose question that helps get right to the heart of the matter in many different situations.

"I just wanted to make sure it's okay."

"That's fine, Mr. Gray."

"Well, is it?"

"Is it what?"

"Is it okay?"

"Yes. Yes, it is. Your toe is fine."

"How come it's all yellow and rough like that?"

"It's because of the fungal infection that you've had for three years."

"Aren't you going to do anything about it?"

"Is it bothering you?"

"Only when I dropped the hammer on it."

It is very important to my patients that I am available to them for urgent conditions like three-year-old fungal infections of the toenail.

A PATIENT RUSHES into the office.

"I don't have an appointment, but I need to see the doctor right away!"

This is the third time this week this woman has appeared in the office demanding an urgent appointment.

She is escorted into an exam room and I join her there shortly.

"What can I do for you today, Ms. Black?"

"Doctor. You have to help me. My heart is racing and pounding like it's going to burst out of my chest! My lungs feel so tight I'm not getting any air at all. My skin is cold and clammy, and I just know I'm going to die!"

When people are in true respiratory distress, they are unable to talk normally. If a patient is really not getting enough air to breathe, she can't get. A complete sentence out. In one breath. She speaks. Slowly and. Carefully. No more. Than one. Or two. Words. At a. Time.

I notice that she is rattling off her symptoms pretty fluently.

"How long have you been feeling like this, Ms. Black?"

"About half an hour, Doctor."

"How old are you now?

"I'm 25."

"That's pretty young for a heart attack or blood clot. Do you smoke, take birth control pills, or have diabetes, high blood pressure, problems with your cholesterol, or a family history of heart attacks or blood clots?"

"No."

"Do you remember the other two panic attacks you've had this week?"

"Yes."

"Does this feel the same?"

"Yes."

"Do you remember having gone to the Emergency Room for them before, Ms. Black?"

"Yes."

"And what did they do for you there?"

"They did an EKG for my heart, a scan of my lungs, and a whole bunch of blood tests."

"Do you remember what they told you?"

"They said there was nothing wrong with my heart or lungs, that I was having a panic attack and that I should see you in the office."

"Do you remember what I did for you then?"

"You ordered a chest x-ray, a stress test, a heart monitor, and more blood tests."

"Do you remember the results?"

"Everything was normal."

"What else did I suggest?"

"That I try counseling and some medication to help with my anxiety."

"Did you go to counseling?"

"No."

"Did you take the medication I prescribed?"

"No."

"Okay then."

The silence between us grows louder. Whoever speaks first loses.

I lose.

"What would you like me to do?"

"I don't know, Doctor, but you have to do something!"

"I can give you a prescription."

"But Doctor, you know how much I hate taking pills."

I wonder how long it will take me to count silently to 100, and whether or not she will still be sitting there staring at me when I'm done.

She is.

"Let me see if I've got this all straight. You've had every medical test I can think of to confirm that your symptoms are not the result of a physical problem of any kind. Those tests were all negative. These episodes are clearly what we call 'panic attacks.' The treatment of panic attacks consists of either counseling, medications, or a combination of both. You don't want to take medication, and you don't want to try counseling. What would you like me to do?"

"I don't know. You're the doctor."

It is at times like these that I wonder if my job would be any easier if I just managed to get more goddamned sleep.

A 15-YEAR-OLD GIRL comes in with abdominal pain. I see her in the office immediately, because abdominal pain can be an emergency.

The definition of "emergency" in the context of abdominal pain is determined by whether or not the patient needs surgery before sunset.

"So tell me about your belly pain."

"It hurts all over my stomach."

"Can you point to where it hurts the most?"

She indicates her belly button.

This is a good start. The closer the pain is to the belly button, the less likely it is to require surgery before sunset.

"How long have you had the pain?"

"About a week."

"Is it getting better, getting worse, or staying the same?"

"It kind of comes and goes, but I guess it's staying the same."

This is continuing to sound good. Most conditions that need surgery before sunset don't go on for a week without changing.

"Are you nauseated at all? Have you thrown up?"

"No."

"Are you hungry?"

"Yes."

This is very good. The kinds of conditions that usually need surgery before sunset involve some kind of intestinal blockage. The digestive tract is a long tube from mouth to anus. If it is blocked anywhere along its length, food starts backing up. The earliest sign of this impending disaster is a loss of appetite, followed by nausea and vomiting.

"When was the last time you pooped?"

"This morning."

Excellent. A blocked digestive tract would not be able to discharge poop.

"When was your last period?"

"Two days ago."

This is also good. She is unlikely to be pregnant.

"Any other symptoms at all? Fever? Sore throat? Burning when you pee? Anything?"

"No."

These are all very good answers. It is increasingly unlikely that she will need surgery before sunset.

"Okay. Let me examine you and we'll see what's going on."

I examine her belly. It is soft. When I put my stethoscope to it, it gurgles. When I press on it, it doesn't hurt anywhere. I examine her everywhere else as well, and find nothing out of the ordinary. I am pleased.

I explain to her why I am pleased.

"I'm pleased to be able to tell you that I find no indication that you will need surgery before sunset."

"Then why does my belly hurt?"

"There are lots of possible reasons. You may have eaten something that disagreed with you, or there may be something bothering you. Sometimes the cause of abdominal pain is emotional. Is there anything bothering you?"

"No."

"Well, it doesn't seem to be that bad, and it doesn't look like you're going to need surgery before sunset."

"Thank you, Doctor."

Another job well done. Or so it seems, until the following day.

It's the same 15-year-old girl with abdominal pain.

"My stomach still hurts."

"Has anything changed?"

"What do you mean?"

"Are you hungry? Have you thrown up? Are you pooping okay? Any other new symptoms?"

"Yes, I'm eating and pooping fine. No, there's nothing else wrong."

I repeat my negative exam. Now it's time to go into a little more detail about any emotional issues. It is clear that this is no longer an emergency.

"Are you sure there's nothing bothering you?"

"Well, my parents are on vacation in Florida."

"Is that upsetting to you?"

"They've never left me before."

I pause, uncertain that I've heard her correctly.

"I beg your pardon?"

"They've never gone anywhere without me before."

"Ever?"

"Ever."

"How long will they be gone?"

"A week. They're coming back tomorrow."

"Are you home alone?"

"No. There's a friend staying with me and my little brother."

"Do you like her?"

"Yes."

"Then, um, what's the problem?"

"They've never left me before!"

"But you're 15 years old."

"So?"

I'm somewhat at a loss for words. But I'm a doctor, so I just say, "Hm," while I think about what to say.

"Don't you think that by age 15 you'd be okay without your parents for one week?"

Now it is her turn to keep silent.

"My stomach hurts," is all she says.

"Well, you don't need surgery before sunset. And your parents will be home tomorrow. You should feel better soon."

Another job well done. Or so it seems, until the next night.

The phone rings in the middle of the night. It is the father of the 15-year-old girl with abdominal pain. He is upset because she is still having abdominal pain. He is especially upset because she is still having abdominal pain despite having seen me not once but twice already, and I have not provided her with a suitable diagnosis.

I explain to him that the important thing about abdominal pain is determining whether or not it needs surgery before sunset—or sunrise, if the sun happens to be down at the time. I explain that both times I saw his daughter I performed a very careful evaluation and was quite confident that she did not have a condition that required surgery before sunset.

I ask if anything has changed.

"What?" he demands.

"Is she eating and moving her bowels? Has the pain changed in character or location? Does she have any other symptoms at all?"

"I don't know. I want her seen again!"

"Now?"

"Now!"

It is now 2:00 in the morning, and I need my goddamned sleep, but I roll out of bed, dress, and meet the family at my office.

They are not happy, but neither am I. I am doing a better job of disguising it, though.

The father is tan but disheveled. The mother is tan; her hair and nails are perfect. The 15-year-old girl with abdominal pain appears to be in no acute distress. I cannot tell if she looks angry, embarrassed, or some combination of both.

Abdominal pain that needs surgery before sunup is often accompanied by abnormal vital signs. Fever is a sign of infection. An elevated pulse and blood pressure are often seen with severe pain. I measure the patient's temperature, pulse, and blood pressure. All are normal.

"Tell me about your pain again," I ask her.

"Like what?"

"Where does it hurt?"

She indicates her belly button.

"Anywhere else?"

"No."

"Have you pooped in the last 12 hours?"

"Yes."

"What was the last thing you had to eat?"

"Pizza."

"When was that?"

"About nine o'clock this evening."

Great. She has indigestion after eating a fatty, spicy pizza right before going to bed.

"Any other symptoms at all?"

"No."

I examine her belly again, inspecting it carefully; it's nice and flat; not distended, which could indicate obstruction. Then I listen with the stethoscope; normal gurgling sounds. Finally I palpate, pushing first gently and then more firmly by turn in each quadrant, watching her face for any sign of discomfort. Nothing. The entire belly is soft, no matter how hard I push. Her belly muscles make no attempt to tense against my hand, either voluntarily or involuntarily. I don't feel anything abnormal inside; no mass that doesn't belong, or any enlargement of the organs that do. I finish with a complete physical examination which is just as normal as her abdominal exam. This child does not need surgery before sunup (which I suddenly realize is now imminent).

"I'm glad to tell you all that she will definitely not need surgery before sunup."

"Then why does her stomach hurt?" demands the father.

Not wanting to embarrass the girl, I pull the parents aside and speak softly.

"I think it's just indigestion from the pizza earlier this evening. You know, 15-year-old girls can be a little dramatic."

The mother stiffens. She pulls herself up to her full five foot, four inches (not counting the three-inch heels). Her eyes blaze at me. If looks could kill, I would be writhing on the floor, blood streaming across the linoleum. She takes an enormous breath and shrieks like a psychotic banshee on megadoses of steroids and with PMS, "Dramatic? Dramatic!?! My daughter is *not* dramatic!!"

POOR PLANNING on your part does not constitute an emergency on my part, even if you think it does. See, *you're* not the one who gets to make the judgment about what constitutes an emergency. *I* do. That's my job.

Sudden onset of crushing chest pain accompanied by shortness of breath, nausea, vomiting, and sweating? Abrupt loss of the ability to speak, see, or walk? Steady waves of muscular contractions as a uterus struggles to expel the products of nine months of development, sending forth a new human into the world? Heart attack; stroke; labor. Now, *those* are emergencies.

"I need an appointment right away for Johnny's sports physical. Practice starts tomorrow and the coach says he can't play unless he has the form signed."

By definition, no preventive care service is an emergency. The fact that Johnny has been carrying the form around in his backpack for the last two months does not convert this into an emergency. Neither does the fact that he is the first-string quarterback upon whose skills the school's entire season rests. Neither does the intransigence of the coach or the school's administration. This is an example of poor planning and nothing more, and poor planning on your part does not constitute an emergency on my part.

## TENTH LAW

# A bad idea held by many people for a long time is still a bad idea.

**B**AD IDEAS HAVE existed ever since the human brain evolved sufficient complexity to allow for creative thought ("Hey, I wonder if saber-toothed tigers like being petted on the nose"), and will likely continue right up until our sun goes super-nova, destroying all life on Earth ("Hey, why did the sun suddenly get so bright? Let's go outside and check it out."). (Technically, the latter is more an example of an irrelevant idea than a bad one, as those who remain inside the house will be fried to identical crispness at virtually the same instant as those who venture outside.) In between those two events—curiosity about the friendliness of saber-toothed cats and the annihilation of the planet—there have been, are, and will continue to be a myriad of very bad ideas held by many people for quite a long time.

In the period of time between the evolution of humanity and the sun's ultimate cosmic demise, though, our sun has been a source of generally more good than bad. The thermodynamic end result of the nuclear reaction of two hydrogen atoms fusing into a single atom of helium (known, conveniently, as "fusion") includes the release of vast amounts of energy. This solar energy escapes into space as heat, light, and radiation of assorted other wavelengths along the electromagnetic spectrum. Eight minutes later a tiny fraction of this radiation lands 93 million miles away on our little planet, where a multitude of organisms have evolved mechanisms both to utilize this energy and to protect themselves from it.

For plants, which utilize solar radiation for food, lying out in the sun is a good idea.

For people, whose more complex genetic material has an annoying susceptibility to damage from that same solar radiation, not so much.

As it happens, humans do need some sunlight absorbed through the skin to produce vitamin D, which is required to absorb calcium, a necessary component of the bones that hold us upright against gravity. This is a good thing.

Unfortunately, solar radiation also has a propensity to knock atoms out of place in other areas of the body that are not involved in the synthesis of vitamin D. Over time, damage can accumulate and cause cancer. This is not a good thing.

Luckily, the body has evolved a protective mechanism against this kind of damage from solar radiation in the form of colored substances, called pigments, that darken when they absorb energy. This is a good thing.

At various times through the history of humanity, the darkening of pigments in the skin has been considered to enhance attractiveness. This is neither a good thing nor a bad thing in and of itself, although it is the source of the quest for the perfect tan (see also: Hamilton, George). For many years this was considered not only harmless, but a good idea. That it is in fact quite a bad idea is only made clear decades later:

"I'm afraid you have skin cancer."

"Oh, no! But I've always had such a great tan! We all enjoyed lying out in the sun when we were younger. Why would something like this happen to me?"

I want to answer, "Because a bad idea held by many people for a long time is still a bad idea," but I refrain.

"Will it leave a scar when you remove the cancer?"

"Yes, I'm afraid it will."

"Will it be very noticeable?"

"Well, scar tissue doesn't have pigment, so it appears lighter on tanned skin."

"Oh, my God. Why did I ever sit out in the sun all those years?"

"I don't know. Why did you?"

"I guess I was just young and stupid."

I've noticed that "young" and "stupid" are often synonymous.

Decades later, the results of long hours in the sun are arrayed across the expanses of skin that now look more like dried-up old leather. As the abnormally growing bits of skin are snipped, shaved, carved, frozen, and biopsied into submission, I believe these patients will never die. I will just keep cutting them away, piece by tiny piece, until there's nothing left.

"I WANT TO BE A DOCTOR."

"Then you'd better take a lot of science courses in college."

"Why can't I study the humanities? After all, I'm going to be taking care of humans."

"Because that's the way it's always been done. The minimum requirements are a year each of general chemistry, organic chemistry, biology, and physics, each with a lab course. Even then, science majors have a tremendous advantage in the medical-school admissions process."

"But most of the science majors I know are more comfortable with numbers and abstract concepts than with people. Maybe that's why so many doctors seem to have such a hard time relating to patients as people instead of just as malfunctioning bodies, if those are the only people who get into medical school."

"That's just the way it's always been done."

"That doesn't sound like a very good idea to me."

It's not. Why should cold, analytical scientists magically morph into compassionate, caring physicians at some point in the course of their training, especially when that training seems designed to stomp out any trace of humanity they may have managed to hang onto through the process?

The issue is being studied, but the process of medical-student selection is still the purview of individual medical schools, a group of institutions that make marble seem flexible. Despite some evidence implying that students with a more varied educational background than hard science end up as adequate or even outstanding physicians, the applicant pool remains top-heavy with science majors.

A bad idea held by many people for a long time is still a bad idea.

ONCE YOU GET INTO medical school, it may not be what you expected.

"Now that I'm here at medical school, I can't wait to meet all the wonderful doctors who are going to teach me everything I need to know to become a great physician."

"Don't hold your breath."

"What do you mean?"

"The only 'doctors' you're going to meet for the first two years are the ones who do medical research."

"What are you talking about?"

"Medical school is all about research. That's where the real prestige is. All the professors are brilliant scientists, famous for their research. I mean, it's not really that hard to provide an overview of the basic subject matter, but it's not why they're here. Teaching medical students is strictly an afterthought."

"But they do teach us, don't they?"

"They like to think so, even though lots of them can't resist the temptation to veer off and tell you all about the latest results of their research."

"So you're saying that they're great in the lab but not so good in the classroom?"

"You didn't hear it from me."

"Why do they do it that way? Why don't they have professors who can teach us what we need to know to take care of patients?"

"They've always done it this way."

Exactly. But a bad idea held by many people for a long time is still a bad idea.

IT'S MY THIRD YEAR of medical school, day one; I'm about to meet real patients for the first time.

A guy in a long, shabby white coat approaches. His hair is mussed and there are bags under his eyes. The pockets of his coat are overflowing with papers, even though one of them contains an electronic digital device that looks like an iPhone. The bottom of his breast pocket is smudged with ballpoint ink. A stethoscope is draped carelessly around his neck.

"Welcome to the wards. I'm your intern. Here, take this chart and go see the patient in that room over there."

An intern? He's only two years ahead of me in training.

"Um, what am I supposed to do?"

"Didn't you learn how to take a history from a patient?"

"Yes, but…"

"Didn't you learn how to do a physical examination?"

"Well, yes, but…"

"So get in there and do a history and physical. And don't forget to do a rectal exam."

"What?"

"I said don't forget to do a rectal exam. Didn't you learn the only two excuses for not doing a rectal exam?"

"No."

"One: no rectum. Two: no finger. Now get going. We have 30 patients on the service and you're presenting yours in one hour."

I am familiar with the noun "service" and the verb "to present," but I get the distinct impression that they mean something else in this context.

"Huh?"

The intern stops and looks at me with annoyance.

"What's wrong with you? There are 30 patients on this hospital floor that our team is responsible for. There's one senior resident, two juniors, and four interns, except that there's only three of us this week while Mike is on vacation."

His voice drips with contempt at the sound of the name "Mike" and the word "vacation" in the same sentence.

"You and the other students on the team divide up the patients and learn everything you can about the ones assigned to you. When we get together for rounds, you present your patients to the attending. And you'd better be prepared!"

And he's off into another patient room before I can catch my breath.

"Wait!" I call after him in vain. "What's wrong with my patient?"

Nothing to do but open the chart and try to decipher the indecipherable handwriting. Or log onto the computer and try to decipher the computer system, which is only marginally decipherable for those training in a different era. Eventually, there's nothing else to do but screw up my courage and march into the patient's room. My very first encounter with an actual patient.

And I'm on my own.

I try to take a history, using notes on little cards that I've prepared for just this occasion, but my mind goes blank. When I start to perform the physical examination, I have no idea where to find an ophthalmoscope or otoscope (for the eye and ear exams, respectively). I do have a little battery-powered penlight for shining into the patient's pupils to see if they contract normally, but I can't get it to work. (Three days later I figure out that it has a little plastic sleeve that must be removed first.) Luckily, I have my own stethoscope draped around my shoulders. I can't quite figure out which way it's more comfortable yet, but it's only the first day.

But I can't for the life of me manage to find a rubber glove and tube of lubricant. My first patient will not be receiving a rectal exam from me today. Besides, I don't even know what I'm supposed to be feeling for.

An hour and a half later, my intern comes looking for me.

"There you are! Come on; we've got rounds."

I follow him up the hall, down a flight of stairs, and into a conference room at the end of another hall. The other members of the team (except Mike, of course) gather around the table and we begin.

The guy at the head of the table turns out to be the senior resident, because he's the one in charge. The other team members take turns rattling off descriptions filled with obscure abbreviations in answer to his queries about the patients. Some of the abbreviations, like AMF, SHPOS, and YOYO make them chuckle. I have no idea what they're talking about. (I later learn that these particular abbreviations are not particularly medical. The "A" in AMF stands for "adios." The "SH" stands for "sub-human," and YOYO means "You're on your own.") Despite what the intern said, I am not called upon to present my patient at this time.

As the meeting breaks up, he turns to me and says, "Have you ever put in a nasogastric tube?"

"No."

"Come on, then."

I follow him to a large storage closet where he begins pulling items off a cart and piling them into my arms. I recognize rubber gloves, a coiled-up plastic tube, and a large syringe with a plastic basin, all sealed individually in paper pouches. The intern, who still hasn't actually introduced himself, though I heard him referred to as "Bob" in the conference room earlier, is talking the entire time.

"Point the tube straight back, like you're trying to pass it right into his brain; not up, the way you think the nose ought to go. It doesn't. He may gag a little as it goes down but just tell him to keep swallowing. That will help pass the tube into the stomach, but you have to keep pushing it. Once it's in the stomach, some stuff may come out the other end."

I look down at my clothes. It's the first time since I've been in medical school that I've worn anything other than jeans and t-shirts. None of the lecturers cared what we wore during the last two years. Hell, fewer than half of the class was ever actually present at any given time, thanks to the note-taking service we had organized. And I had thrown away the oldest, rattiest jeans and shirt I owned after wearing them specifically for gross anatomy lab. We all had. We wanted to have a big party where we got together and burned them ceremonially, but the fumes would have been too toxic. The skirt and blouse I had on today weren't anything special, but they were new.

"Do I have time to change into scrubs first?"

Bob rolls his eyes and grabs back all the stuff he'd piled in my arms.

"Never mind. I'll do it myself."

"Wait! Wait, I'll do it."

He pays no attention to me as he storms off to the patient's room. I follow and watch as he unwraps his things and lays them out on a table next to the bed. He douses the end of the tube with clear jelly from a small blue foil pack (the location of which I have now made note, for future rectal exams) and grabs the top of the patient's head with one hand as he begins shoving the tube into the man's nose with his other, yelling at him to swallow the entire time. The patient is gagging and struggling, but he's too old and weak to put up much of a fight. Even I can tell that his belly is hugely distended, though, so he clearly needs the tube for decompression. (In later years, clinical research began to show that gastrointestinal tubes weren't nearly as effective as everyone thought they were. Not only is a bad idea held by many people for a long time still a bad idea, but, as mentioned, half of what we're taught in medical school is wrong and no one knows which half.) The length of tubing at the patient's nose is disappearing rapidly as Bob continues to shove it in. Suddenly there is a gush of brownish fluid from the open end. Bob avoids getting splashed with it as he aims the tube toward the plastic basin he has set in front of the patient.

I watch as Bob attaches the large syringe to the end of the tube and proceeds to suction more of the brownish fluid out of the patient's stomach. Bob detaches the syringe and squirts its contents into the basin. When he is through, he connects the tube to a small pump sitting on a stand at the bedside. I watch as he pins the tube to the patient's hospital gown and then walks out, leaving the mess of the syringe and basin, now full of brownish fluid, for a nurse's aide to clean up. I notice a few splashes of fluid on the patient's gown, and hope that someone brings him a new one.

"Hey! Where are you?" I hear Bob calling.

I scurry to join him at the nurse's station, where he has the chart open to a blank page.

"Here's how we document that." My mind wanders as he rattles off the technical details of the procedure I've just witnessed, wondering how the patient felt about having a tube shoved through his nose into his stomach.

"You'll do the next one."

"What?"

"Next time, you'll do it. You've seen it done, so now you're ready to do it yourself."

"Is that all it takes?"

"Yep. See one, do one, teach one. That's how it works. We've always done it that way."

I'm too intimidated by everything that's happened so far on my first day of clinical medicine to protest, but I'm pretty sure that "see one, do one, teach one" is a bad idea, even though it's been held by many people for a long time.

Over the next few days I learn all kinds of things. I learn how to draw blood. I learn how to locate x-ray reports. I finally learn how to pass a nasogastric tube—although I never quite get the hang of aiming the open end into the basin, so I usually get splashed with the brownish fluid that comes out of it. Luckily, I learn where the scrubs are kept and remember to change into them before passing nasogastric tubes.

Very little of what I'm learning seems to have anything to do with medicine. There are long-winded, esoteric discussions of diagnosis and treatment at rounds every morning as we sit around the big table together, but few specifics; at least none that I can comprehend at this stage of my training. Most of my time is spent on menial tasks. I become an expert at drawing blood and the woman in the x-ray department's film room is my new best friend. I am learning to write progress notes in patient charts, but the intern always has to countersign them. Someone else also has to countersign my orders, but it's kind of a joke. I have no idea what to order, so I act as a scribe while the intern or one of the residents rattles off orders for tests and treatments. I barely understand what's being said, let alone what it means and why it's being done.

I learn that there is actually a term for these menial tasks that are so vital to patient care but so mind-numbingly dull to perform. It is called "scut work." It's the perfect term; almost an expletive, yet subliminally scatological. I don't see how these tasks advance my medical education, yet I dare not say anything. Clearly, this is the way things have been done for a long time, even though it seems like a bad idea held by many people.

Later that week, an attending—a fully trained physician who actually knows what he's doing—shows up, gathers all six of us students who are on the rotation, and takes us back into the conference room in which we'd met without him that morning. For the next blessed hour, he answers all the basic, nuts-and-bolts questions none of us have had the nerve to ask the interns and residents who have been running us ragged all day. All the minutiae of the tubes, fluids, and how a hospital unit is run are finally explained in a stress-free, ridicule-free environment. He then takes us back to see several patients and review their physical findings. Hearts with murmurs, lungs with crackles, and bellies with fluid are demonstrated, so that finally we understand what our earlier professors were trying to teach us about physical exam techniques.

Later, talking with friends on other rotations at other hospitals, even in the same hospital but on different floors, I discover that not all were so lucky. The idea that bedside teaching, recognized as both a time-honored tradition and the bastion of an effective medical education, should be left to the randomness by which an attending may or may not take pity on us is surely a bad idea, despite apparently being held by many people for a long time.

AS MY THIRD YEAR progresses, things get somewhat easier. I learn where to find things and how to get things done. I learn how to examine a patient in a rumpled hospital bed instead of on a pristine examination table. I learn to carry what I need, and soon the pockets of my short white coat are as stretched out as the interns'.

I learn more about rounds, and as I do, I begin to appreciate more of the subtle nuances between the players.

The senior resident is in charge. He is the one with the ultimate responsibility for all the patients, so he has to know everything that is going on at all times. Later—much later—I learn that it is actually the attending who has the legal responsibility for supervising even the senior resident. But at this stage of my training, I know so little compared to the senior that he may as well be God. Once I have multiple rotations under my belt, I learn that some seniors are more friendly and approachable than others. Those willing to answer our "dumb" questions are worshipped; the frostier ones are avoided whenever possible.

The junior residents vary similarly in their approaches to us. Some just want to get their work done and go home, while others seem more willing to teach.

The interns are the workhorses. Although we students

are supposedly the bottom of the heap, the interns are the ones who get the heat if and when we screw up. They're also the most tired, though it seems to me their fatigue comes more from the anxiety of uncertainty than their absolute workload—although after a long, hard day with lots of new patients on the service to work up, everyone is testy.

But it is at rounds where I begin to notice something more pernicious.

There comes a time each morning when the team gathers with the attending. Different attendings prefer different times, but it is almost always sometime in the morning. There is a tension in the air as the interns begin to present the patients.

"This is an 80-year-old white male originally admitted with an exacerbation of his chronic obstructive pulmonary disease, found to have a new lung mass diagnosed as a small-cell lung carcinoma," an intern might begin. She will continue with details of the patient's symptoms and findings when he first came to the hospital, followed by a recitation of what had been done for him here and what other tests had showed. When she is done—if the attending lets her finish; some were notorious for jumping in after the first sentence or two—the questions begin.

"What is the differential diagnosis of lung nodules? What characteristics of lung nodules would make you suspicious for a malignancy? What other physical findings might you expect to find in a patient with lung cancer?"

The questioning is merciless, and stops only when the student, intern, or resident gets an answer wrong. The worst response is, "I don't know." This is often followed with a tongue-lashing about how basic and elementary the question is, and usually results in the assignment of a talk on the subject the following day by the disgraced individual, "so that everyone can learn more about this."

Next, the junior and senior residents are grilled about their choices of patient management options. Decisions are endlessly hashed, re-hashed, debated, and second-guessed. The only certainty is that the trainee could have done better. Needless to say, I quickly grew to dread being called upon in rounds, because even when I thought I knew what I was doing, I knew I'd never be good enough.

THERE ARE LARGE quantities of data showing that people, specifically adults, learn best in a supportive milieu of positive feedback, so why does this style of education persist? Emotional abuse that is perpetuated by one generation of physicians on the next and continues in the name of tradition is nothing but a bad idea held by many people for a long, long time.

ALTHOUGH MEDICAL training seems like it's never going to end, eventually it does. The next step is going out into the world to earn a living as a doctor.

Earning a living involves money.

You suddenly realize that the relationship between medicine and money has never actually been discussed in the last seven (or more) years. Oh, you got a paycheck during residency, but it wasn't all that much. You were still learning, after all. But all that is different now, and you're on your own. Medical training taught you how to practice medicine. Now you have to learn to get paid for it.

Why not go out, find an office to rent, buy some equipment, and, literally, hang out a shingle?

I did exactly that.

So where does the money come from?

Most people borrow some to get started with the initial equipment purchases and operating expenses. Once the patients start walking in the door, though, it's showtime.

In any other service profession, you set fees and collect them from clients. But not medicine. No. For reasons that are truly unfathomable, the American public labors under the assumption that medical care is paid for through assorted third parties.

It all started a long time ago as a reasonable idea to help spread the risk of financially ruinous medical bills among a large pool of healthy people, and was called "hospitalization insurance." It was originally intended to cover catastrophic expenses associated with a major illness, accident, or surgery, and, in the days of Marcus Welby, that's what it did. Patients paid their doctors out of their own pockets. Sometimes their insurance plans reimbursed them, but by and large, patients understood that the insurance contract was an agreement between themselves and the insurance company.

Then the insurance companies decided that contracting directly with the doctors could be lucrative. They offered the doctors a steady stream of patients by advertising for them among patients with certain insurance coverage, in exchange for the doctors giving discounts on their fees and submitting their charges directly to the company. Patients loved the convenience. Instead of the patient paying the doctor in the office, the doctor just billed the insurance company for the patient's treatment. All the patient owed was a small co-pay. Such a deal!

Apparently, most of the doctors back then thought the direct connection with insurance companies was a pretty good deal too. Instead of billing all their patients individually—because of course not everyone actually paid in the office—doctors just had the insurance companies to deal with.

It was a sweet deal for the insurance companies. They collected premiums from the patients (or their employers) and processed claims from the doctors. The insurance industry makes its money when premiums in are greater than claims paid out.

But health insurance isn't really "insurance." Think about home or auto insurance. The idea is to protect you against catastrophe, not to pay for upkeep. You pay your car insurance premium and hope you never need the policy.

Have you ever gotten into your car and said, "I'm going to go out and crash this thing, because my auto insurance premiums are terribly expensive and by God I'm going to get my money's worth of it!"? I don't think so.

But as preventive medical care grows in popularity, and as health-insurance policies cover visits to the doctor for any reason, the insurance company's profit is squeezed. That will never do—for them—so something's got to give. Premiums go up and claims paid to doctors go down.

What's the big deal for the doctor? It's just a contract. It's a free country. Contracts can always be negotiated. If an insurance company doesn't pay you enough, you don't sign the contract. Simple, right?

Would that it were so.

You, the doctor, have to attract customers—though we call them patients—if you are to stay in business. There's just no way around this simple fact of economic life. If you don't sign the insurance contract, you are not considered a "participating" physician by that company. And in this day and age, Americans will not see a physician if he doesn't take their insurance. Patients pay outrageous premiums, so they need to get their money's worth! Why should they see a doctor they have to pay directly when they can see a different doctor who accepts payment from their insurance company?

It sometimes seems that the patient-doctor relationship is dead. Not the doctor-patient relationship. That's the one I treasure, with patients I've known and nurtured for years.

The patient-doctor relationship, though, is apparently no longer worth anything more than an insurance co-pay to many patients. If a doctor stops participating with an insurance company, his patients flock like lemmings to the next office up the street that does. The new doctor may be brusque and the office may be too busy to return patients' phone calls, but it only costs a $15 co-pay.

The logical question here is: Can't the doctor just negotiate a more favorable contract?

I can try:

"Hello, I'm Dr. Welby. I'm a participating physician with your insurance company, and my expenses have gone up so I'd like to negotiate an increase in the rates you pay me to take care of patients you cover."

"Certainly, Dr. Welby. How many physicians are in your practice?"

"One."

"I beg your pardon?"

"Just one. Me. I'm in solo practice."

"Oh. I see. May I ask how many patients you have?"

"Currently I have about 200 active patients covered through your company."

"Um, Dr. Welby, we have over a million covered lives in your metropolitan area alone. We have hundreds of other doctors willing to accept our rates. It makes no sense for us to negotiate with you for higher payment. If you don't like our contract, you don't have to sign it."

"But what about my patients?"

"They'll have to find another doctor who does participate. There are dozens of them in your zip code alone. Or
they can continue to see you and pay you directly."

"But I want to negotiate my contract with you."

"I'm sorry, Dr. Welby. You really don't have anything
with which to negotiate."

FAMILY DOCTORS like me are being starved out of practice
by the shrinking payments of a failed model of health insurance. Marcus Welby himself would be the first to agree
that a bad idea held by many people for a long time is still
a bad idea.

# The Bill of Wrongs

SOME THINGS never change. Humans are born, grow up, reproduce, fall ill, and eventually die. Over the millennia, medical marvels have been developed that have made each of these phases of life safer and healthier. Certainly they have lengthened the overall life span, and there is no doubt that modern medicine is to thank for that, regardless of its foibles. Still, people are fundamentally the same, and they want the same things from their lives: freedom from suffering and pain for both themselves and their families, and compassion and empathy from caring professionals when pain and suffering cannot be avoided. This was where Marcus Welby excelled; it was his calling, as it is mine.

Yet here I am, a modern-day family physician, an heir of Marcus Welby, declaring myself to be a dinosaur; a magnificent creature (I say, modestly) at the brink of extinction due to factors beyond my control. What are some of these factors, and what, if anything can be done to prevent the loss of my profession forever?

FIRST: Banish Preauthorization

I am the one whose training and experience has prepared me to diagnose and treat patients. Ordering diagnostic studies such as x-rays, CT, MRI, and cardiac imaging is an integral part of what I do. Forcing me to justify my decisions to untrained clerks reading off a computer screen is unnecessary, insulting, and a waste of time.

SECOND: Close the Liability Lottery

Listening to late-night television is a risk factor for development of the disease known as "Entitlementitis." The idea that those who suffer illnesses and injuries which medicine may not be able to treat satisfactorily—the general misfortunes of life, that is—deserve monetary compensation is probably the most pernicious wedge that has been driven between patients and doctors. It turns every interaction into a potential conflict, and is the driving force behind the massive overtesting and overtreatment that differentiates Marcus Welby's practice from medicine today. Find a way to bring patients and doctors back together as allies instead of enemies.

### THIRD: Control Quackery

Vitamins won't cure cancer and there is no magic weight-loss pill. People must accept that there is no such thing as magic. At the very least, patients should be protected against those who lie to them to steal their money. Terms such as "alternative," "complementary," and "integrative" medicine should be eliminated and the practices called what they really are: quackery.

### FOURTH: Respect My Skills

Dear Dr. Specialist: Just because you know everything there is to know about the left nostril does not make you better than me, even if your residency training was twice as long as mine. We all have important roles in patient care, but you disparage my clinical skills by sending patients hither and yon to other specialists, each of whom does extensive (and expensive, and unnecessary) workups, instead of back to me. "More" is not always "better." Not everyone with high blood pressure needs a cardiologist, and not everyone with a headache needs a neurosurgeon. The diminishing respect that family practitioners receive from specialist colleagues is disheartening and frustrating.

FIFTH: Show Me the Money

Medicine is a calling, but I also have bills to pay. Why is an hour of my time spent talking to a patient, examining him, and explaining the diagnosis and treatment plan worth one-sixth of what a specialist may receive for a five-minute procedure? Physician payment needs massive restructuring, because as a profession, family practice is rapidly becoming no longer financially viable in this country.

THESE ARE JUST a few of the environmental factors driving my species to extinction. There's no giant meteor striking the planet and producing cataclysmic devastation; rather, it's a gradual picking away of my habitat, my food supply, my environment, my way of life. Rising in my place are new breeds of doctors, expert at caring for tiny, specific parts of the body but incapable of tending to the whole person. These new breeds roam the clinical plains in massive herds, because there is safety in numbers. None, they fear, can stand alone against the coming storms. For the moment, I remain.

There are others like me; more than you may think. We toil away, one by one in our solo offices, hidden away from the toxic influences threatening to devour us, coping as best we can. One by one we have been succumbing, but those who remain continue along our tried and true course:

ministering to our patients one at a time, listening, diagnosing, treating, and comforting.

As a solo family doctor I may indeed be going the way of the dinosaur, but I'm not dead yet.